10-MINUTE

BRAIN GAMES

LOGIC AND REASONING

About the Author

Dr Gareth Moore is the internationally best-selling author of a wide range of brain-training and puzzle books for both children and adults, including *Anti-stress Puzzles, Ultimate Dot to Dot, Brain Games for Clever Kids, Lateral Logic* and *Extreme Mazes.* His books have sold over a million copies in the UK alone, and have been published in 29 different languages. He is also the creator of online brain-training site BrainedUp.com, and runs daily puzzle site PuzzleMix.com.

10-MINUTE

BRAIN GAMES

LOGIC AND REASONING

Michael O'Mara Books Limited

First published in Great Britain in 2018 by
Michael O'Mara Books Limited
9 Lion Yard
Tremadoc Road
London SW4 7NQ

A CIP catalogue record for this book is available from the British Library.

Papers used by Michael O'Mara Books Limited are natural, recyclable products made from wood grown in sustainable forests. The manufacturing processes conform to the environmental regulations of the country of origin.

ISBN: 978-1-78243-905-9 in paperback print format

1 2 3 4 5 6 7 8 9 10

www.mombooks.com
www.drgarethmoore.com

Designed and typeset by Gareth Moore
Printed and bound by CPI Group (UK) Ltd, Croydon, CR0 4YY

▪ Introduction ▪

Welcome to *10-Minute Brain Games: Logic and Reasoning*, packed from cover to cover with many different types of logic and reasoning puzzle, all designed to be solvable in around 10 minutes or so.

There's a handy area on each page for keeping track of your solving time. Unless you are already familiar with a particular type of puzzle, then the chances are that the first time you tackle it you won't manage to solve it in 10 minutes, so don't worry if you start off (much) slower! It's simply a target time for each puzzle, and by the end of the book you may well have brought down your solving times on many of the puzzles. You'll be able to find out by flicking back to see the times you noted down earlier on, so it's worth starting at the beginning and working through.

Full instructions for each and every puzzle are conveniently located at the bottom of each page, with a sentence or paragraph to give the basic aim and then some bullet points to specify the finer rules of that particular type. If any of the rules seem confusing, take a quick glance at the solution and work out how the clues correspond to the final result. Many of the puzzles have similar basic mechanics, such as drawing loops or paths, or placing numbers, so even if you find it a little confusing at first do persevere because you'll soon get into the swing of things.

Full solutions are at the back of the book, should you need them to help you, or simply wish to check your answer.

Good luck, and have fun!

▪ Arrow Sudoku ▪

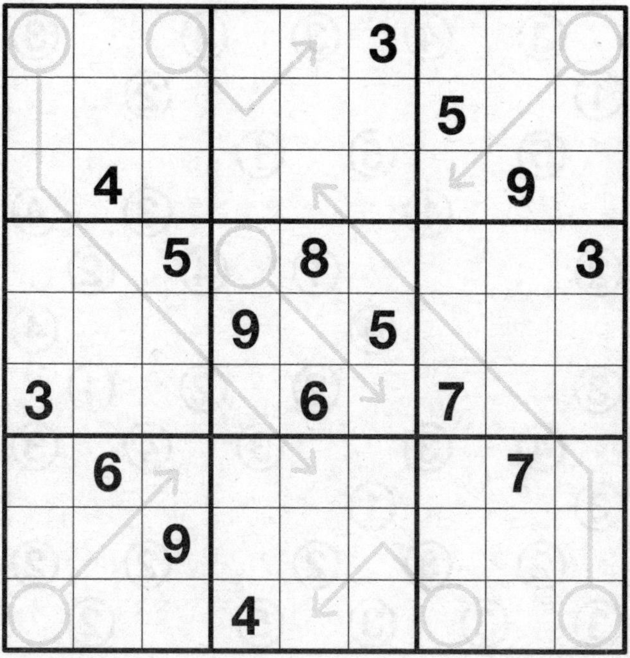

Instructions

Place a digit from 1 to 9 into every empty square, so that each digit appears once in every row, column and bold-lined 3×3 box.

- Circled squares must contain a value equal to the sum of the digits along their attached arrows.

Your solving time: ____________

▪ Bridges ▪

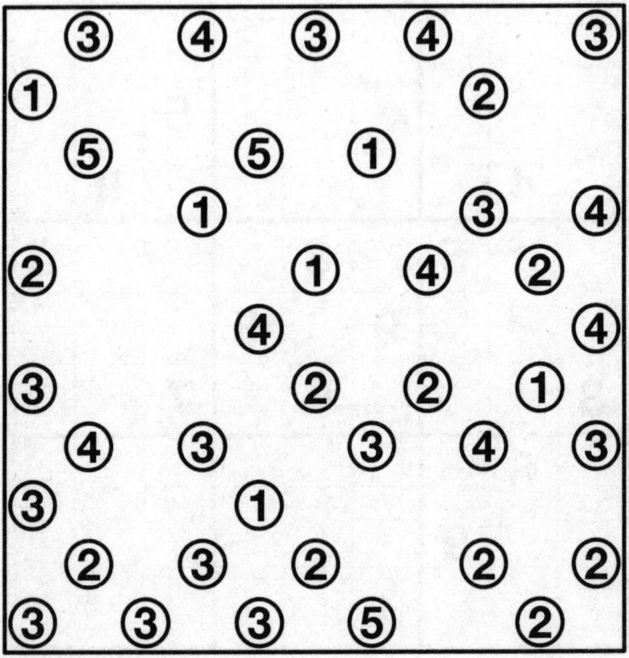

Instructions

Draw horizontal and vertical lines to represent bridges joining pairs of islands. Islands are indicated by circled numbers, where the number specifies the number of bridges that connect to that island.

- Any pair of islands may be joined by up to two bridges.
- Bridges may not cross either another bridge or an island.
- All islands must be joined together by the bridges, so you can travel to any island just by following the bridges.

Your solving time: ____________

▪ Kropki ▪

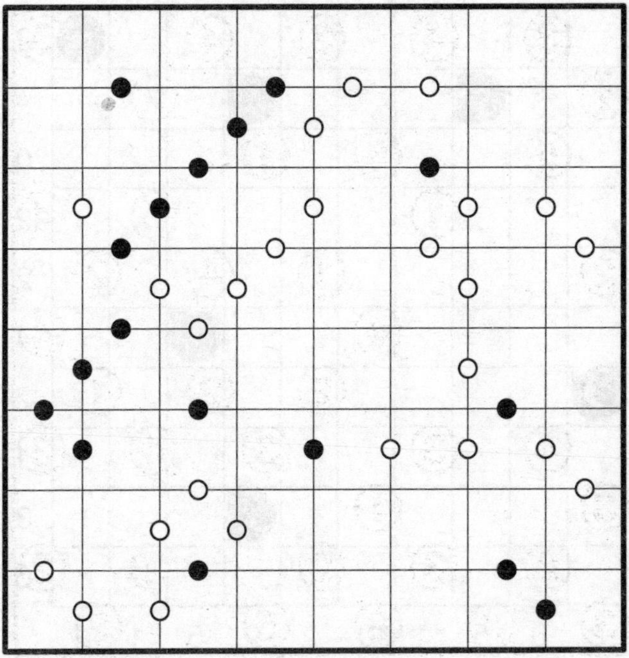

Instructions

Place digits from 1 to 8 once each in every row and column.

- Squares separated by a white dot must contain two consecutive numbers, such as 2 and 3, or 5 and 6.
- Squares separated by a black dot must contain numbers where one is twice the value of the other, such as 2 and 4.
- All possible dots are given – except where both a black and a white dot could be given, in which case only one dot is shown. The absence of a dot is therefore significant.

Your solving time: ____________

▪ Battleships ▪

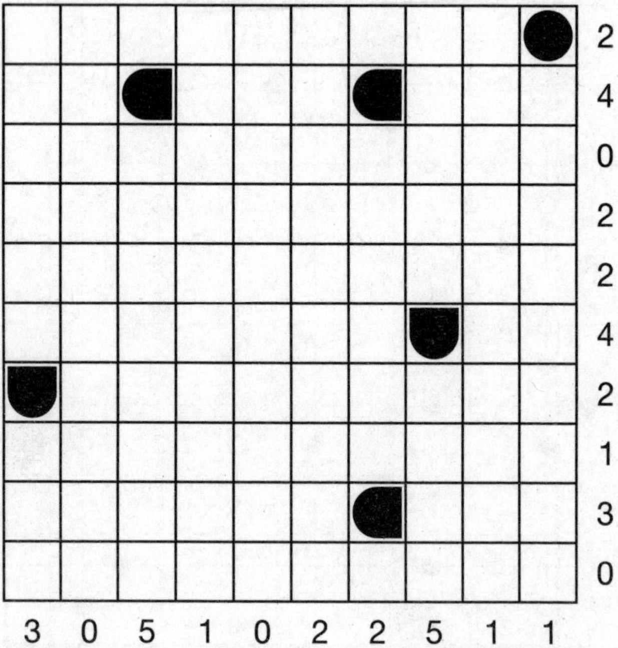

Instructions

Place the given set of 10 ships into the grid.

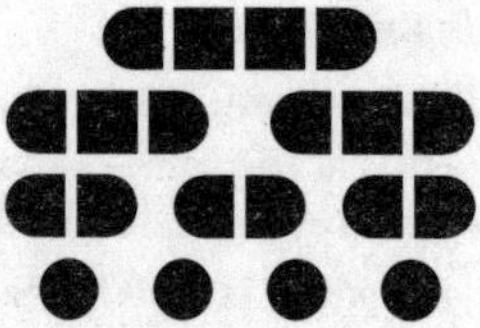

- Clues outside the grid reveal the number of squares in the corresponding row or column that contain a ship part.
- Ships cannot touch each other – not even diagonally.
- Some ship parts are already placed.
- Ships cannot be placed diagonally.

 Your solving time: ____________

▪ Snake ▪

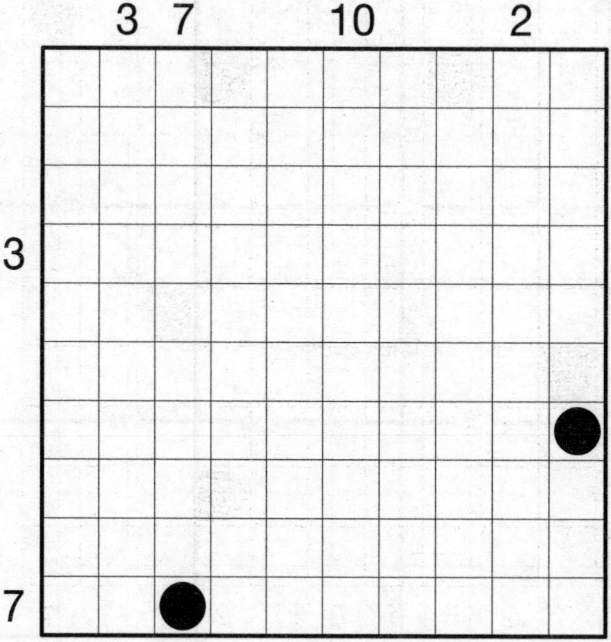

Instructions

Shade some squares to form a single snake that starts and ends at the squares marked with circles.

- A snake is a path of adjacent squares that does not branch or cross over itself.
- The snake does not touch itself – not even diagonally, except when turning a corner.
- Numbers outside the grid reveal the number of squares in their row or column that contain part of the snake.

Your solving time: _____________

▪ Quad Pencil-mark Sudoku ▪

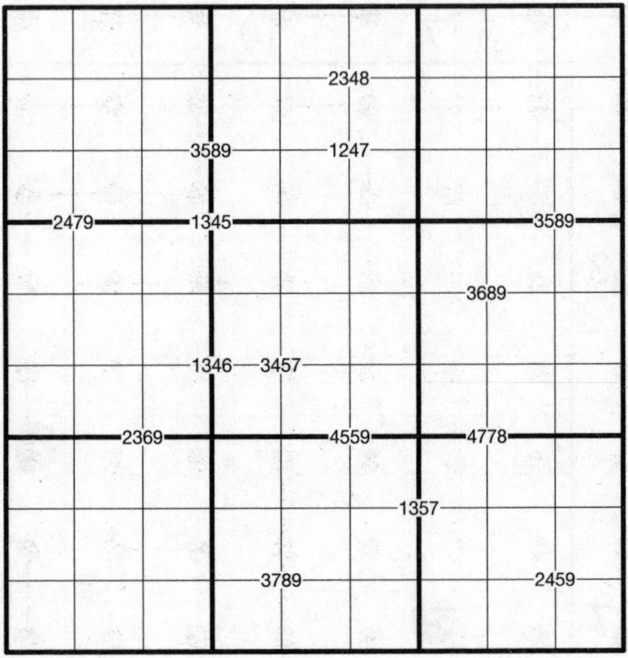

Instructions

Place a digit from 1 to 9 into every square, so that each digit appears once in every row, column and bold-lined 3×3 box.

- Wherever four digits appear on the intersection of four squares, those digits must be placed into those four squares in some order.

 Your solving time: ____________

▪ Fences ▪

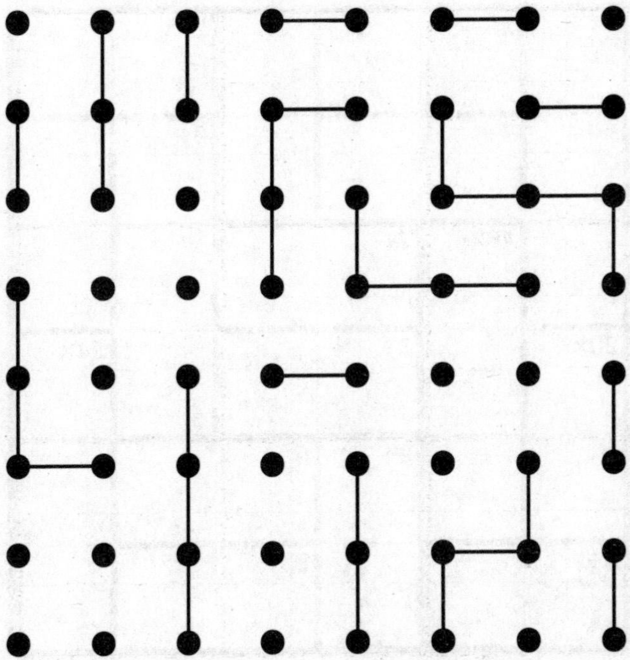

Instructions

Join all of the dots so as to form a single loop.

- The loop does not cross over or touch itself at any point.
- The loop can only consist of horizontal and diagonal lines between dots.

Your solving time: ______________

▪ Calcudoku ▪

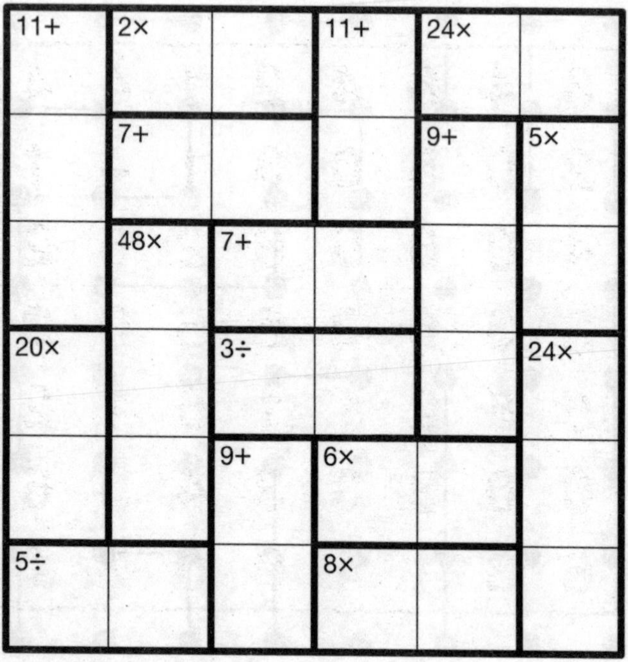

Instructions

Place a digit from 1 to 6 into every square, so that no digit repeats in any row or column.

- The value at the top-left of each bold-lined region must result when all of the numbers in that region have the given operation (+, –, ×, ÷) applied between them. For – and ÷ operations begin with the largest number in the region and then subtract or divide by the other numbers in any order.

 Your solving time: ____________

▪ Dominoes ▪

6	4	6	4	2	1	4	4
2	0	5	0	3	1	4	1
4	0	6	5	6	2	5	2
3	3	6	2	6	5	0	2
5	5	2	1	1	5	1	2
0	0	3	3	3	4	5	6
6	3	1	4	0	0	3	1

Instructions

Draw solid lines to divide the grid up to form a complete set of standard dominoes, with exactly one of each domino.

- A '0' represents a blank on a traditional domino.
- Use the check-off chart to help you keep track of which dominoes you've placed.

0	1	2	3	4	5	6	
							0
							1
							2
							3
							4
							5
							6

Your solving time: ____________

▪ King's Journey ▪

35		37		55	60		
					57		
	33		49			1	64
32						42	
21		27				43	
19			25	46		4	
17			24		11		8

Instructions

Write a number in each of the empty squares so that the grid contains every number from 1 to 64 exactly once.

- Place the numbers so that there is a route from 1 to 64 that visits every grid square exactly once in increasing numerical order, moving only left, right, up, down or diagonally between touching squares.

 Your solving time: ____________

▪ Skyscrapers ▪

				3		
						4
2						1
4						
	1					

Instructions

Place a digit from 1 to 5 into every square, so that no digit repeats in any row or column inside the grid.

- Each clue number outside the grid gives the number of digits that are 'visible' from that point, looking along that clue's row or column. A digit is visible unless there is a higher digit preceding it, reading from the clue along the row or column. E.g. the clue to the left of 14235 would be 3, since 1, 4 and 5 are visible, but 2 and 3 are obscured by 4.

Your solving time: ____________

▪ Four in a Row ▪

X		O	O	O			X
O	O				X	X	X
	O	O					O
O	O	O		O	O		X
						X	
O	X			O		X	O
		X					O
	X		X		X	X	O

Instructions

Place either an × or an o into every empty square.

- Complete the grid *without* forming any lines of four or more ×s or os.
- Lines can be formed in horizontal, vertical and diagonal directions.

Your solving time: ____________

▪ Slitherlink ▪

3	3	3	3	2	2	3	3
1		1		0			1
3	2		3	1			2
2		2		0		1	3
3	3		3		3		2
2			2	1		3	2
3			2		2		1
3	2	3	3	2	3	3	3

Instructions

Draw a single loop by connecting together some, but not necessarily all, dots so that each numbered square has the specified number of adjacent line segments.

- Dots can only be joined by horizontal or vertical lines.
- The loop cannot touch, cross or overlap itself in any way.

Your solving time: ____________

▪ Walls ▪

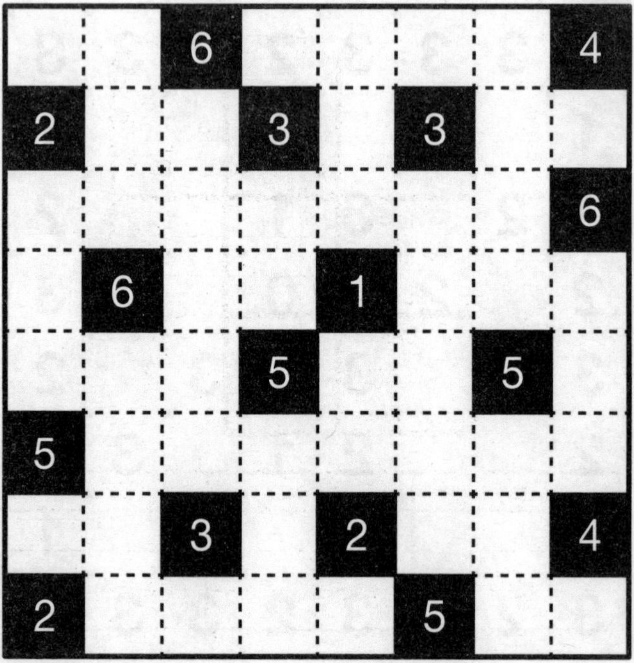

Instructions

Draw a horizontal or vertical line across the full width or height of the centre of every white square.

- The total length of all lines touching each black square must be equal to the number printed on that cell.
- The length of a line is defined as the number of squares it covers.
- Some lines may be shared between black squares; other lines may not touch any black squares.

Your solving time: ____________

▪ Written Logic ▪

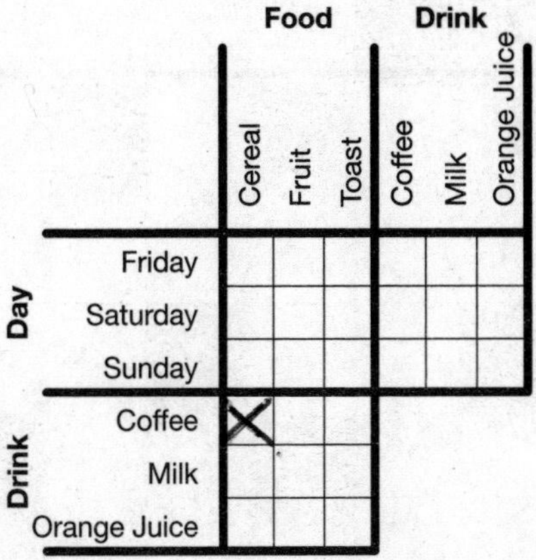

Day	Food	Drink

Breakfast Time

Last Friday, Saturday and Sunday, you had a different breakfast every day, with a choice of fruit, cereal and toast. You also had a choice of drink, with coffee, milk, and orange juice to choose from. What food and drink did you have for breakfast each day, given the following facts?

- You ate cereal the day before you drank milk.
- You drank orange juice before the day you ate fruit.
- You had a one-word drink with your bowl of cereal.

Your solving time: ____________

▪ Path Finder ▪

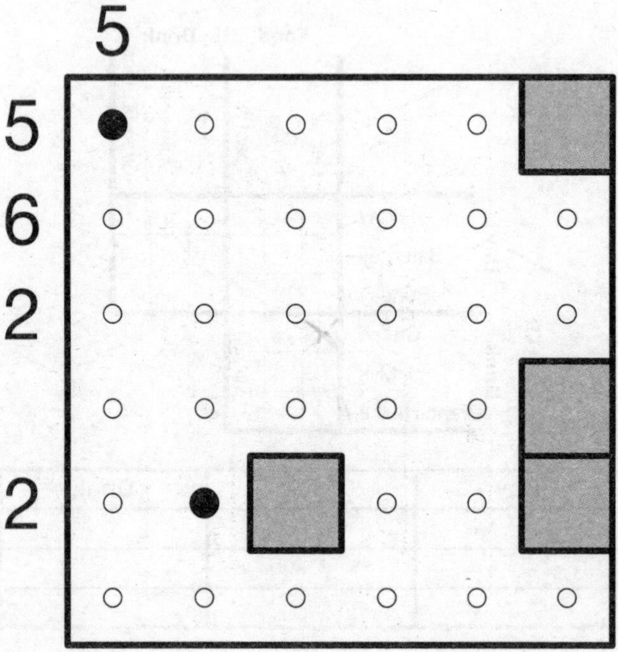

Instructions

Join some of the dots to form a single path which does not touch or cross itself at any point.

- The start and end of the path are indicated by black dots.
- Numbers outside the grid specify the number of dots in their row or column that are visited by the path.
- The path can't touch or cross over any of the shaded boxes.
- The path is constructed only of horizontal and vertical line segments.

 Your solving time: ____________

▪ Sudoku 3D Star ▪

Instructions

Place a digit from 1 to 8 into each empty square, so that no digit repeats in any row or column of 8 squares, or any bold-lined 4×2 or 2×4 box.

- Rows and columns start at one edge of the grid and follow along the same row or column until they reach half way across the grid; then they bend with the 3D surface and continue until they reach a different edge of the grid.

Your solving time: ____________

▪ Loop Finder ▪

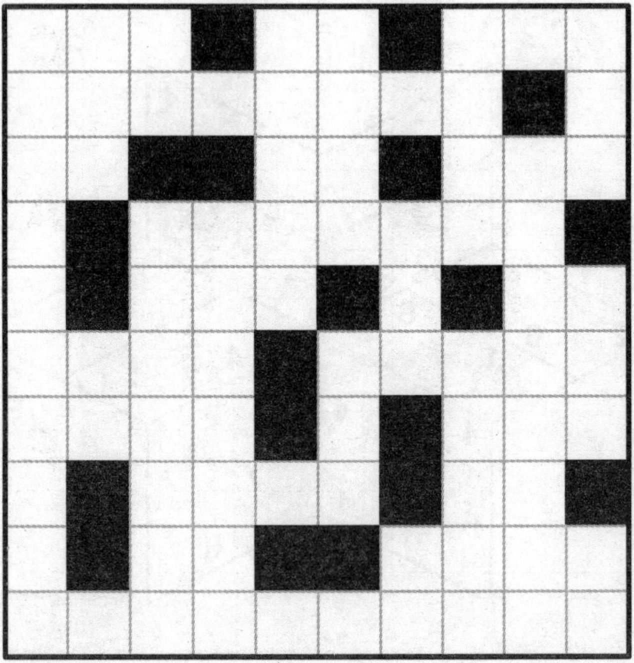

Instructions

Draw a single loop which visits every white square exactly once.

- The loop cannot touch or cross over either itself or a black square at any point.
- The loop consists only of horizontal and vertical line segments.

Your solving time: ____________

▪ Touchy ▪

A							C
B		D			G		A
	F	C			B	E	
	A	E			H	C	
C		G			A		F
D							B

Instructions

Place a letter from A to H into every square, so that no letter repeats in any row or column.

- Identical letters cannot be in diagonally touching squares.

Your solving time: ____________

▪ Frame Sudoku ▪

	7	5	9	6	6	9	
6							15
15							6
8							13
13							8
7							14
14							7
	10	5	6	4	10	7	

Instructions

Place a digit from 1 to 6 into every square, so that no digit repeats in any row or column.

- Clue numbers outside the grid give the sum of all the digits that are in the adjacent 3×2 box *and* that are in the same row or column as the clue.

 Your solving time: ____________

▪ Binary Placement ▪

			0			1	1
0	1					1	1
			0			0	
			0		0		1
1		1		0			
	0			1			
1	1					1	0
1	1			0			

Instructions

Place 0 or 1 in every empty square so that there are an equal number of each digit in every row and column.

- Reading along any row or column, there must not be more than two of the same digit in direct succession. For example, 10011001 would be a valid row, while 10001101 would not be valid due to the three 0s in direct succession.

Your solving time: ____________

▪ Hanjie ▪

						5	4	3	2	1
	1	2	3	3	10	3	3	3	2	1
1										
2										
3										
4										
5										
6										
1										
10										
8										
6										

Clue: Afloat

Instructions

Shade some squares while obeying the clues at the start of each row or column.

- The clues provide, in reading order, the length of every run of consecutive shaded squares in each row and column.
- There must be a gap of at least one empty square between each run of shaded squares in the same row or column.
- The finished puzzle will reveal a simple picture which fits the clue given beneath.

Your solving time: ____________

▪ Number Link ▪

			1						
	2		3					3	
4				5					
6									
	2								
				7					
8		4		9	8		9		
				6			1		
								7	5

Instructions

Draw a set of separate paths, with one path connecting each pair of identical numbers.

- No more than one path can enter any square, and paths can only travel horizontally or vertically between squares.
- Paths cannot touch or cross one another.

Your solving time: ___________

▪ Kakuro ▪

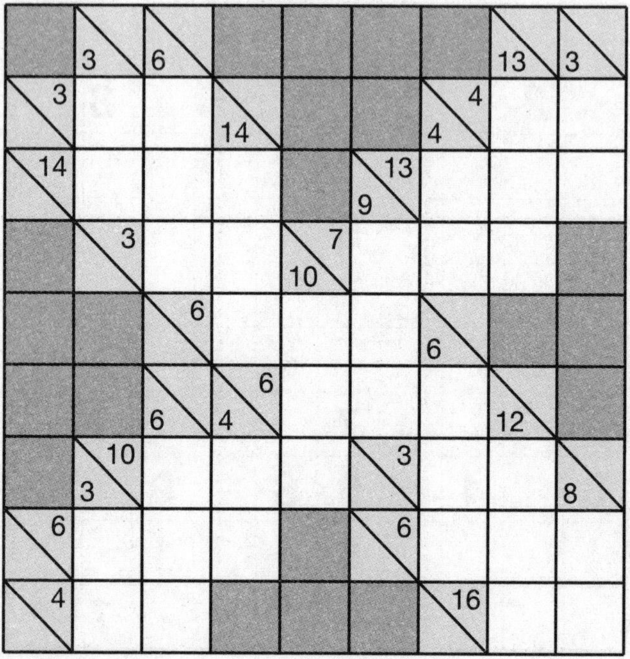

Instructions

Place a digit from 1 to 9 into each white square, and so that no placed digit repeats in any consecutive horizontal or vertical 'run' of squares.

- Each horizontal or vertical 'run' has a total given immediately to its left or above respectively. The digits in that run must add up to the given total.

Your solving time: ______________

▪ Arrow Sudoku ▪

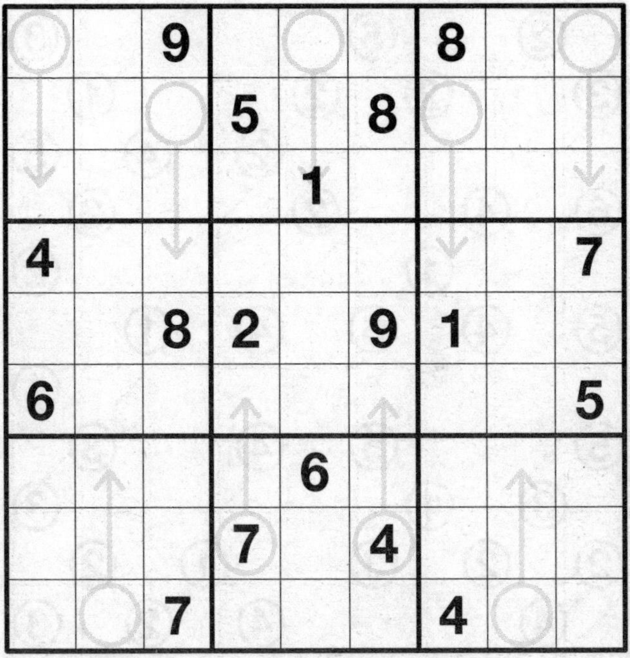

Instructions

Place a digit from 1 to 9 into every empty square, so that each digit appears once in every row, column and bold-lined 3×3 box.

- Circled squares must contain a value equal to the sum of the digits along their attached arrows.

Your solving time: ____________

▪ Bridges ▪

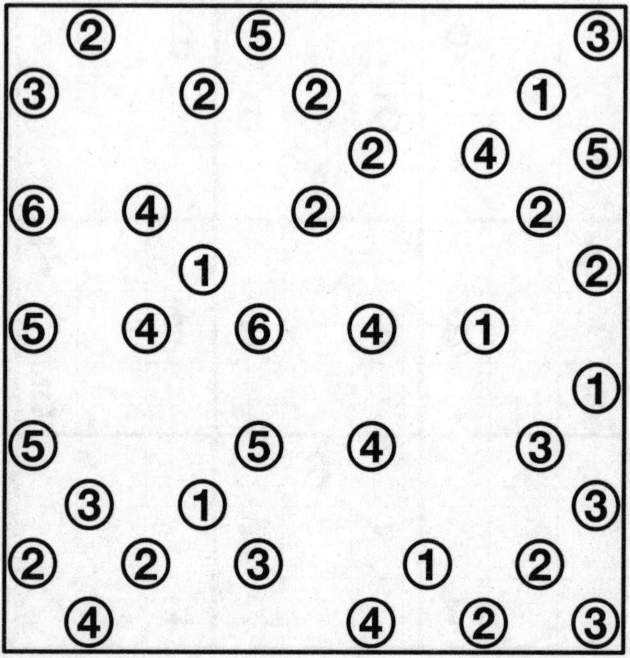

Instructions

Draw horizontal and vertical lines to represent bridges joining pairs of islands. Islands are indicated by circled numbers, where the number specifies the number of bridges that connect to that island.

- Any pair of islands may be joined by up to two bridges.
- Bridges may not cross either another bridge or an island.
- All islands must be joined together by the bridges, so you can travel to any island just by following the bridges.

Your solving time: ____________

▪ Kropki ▪

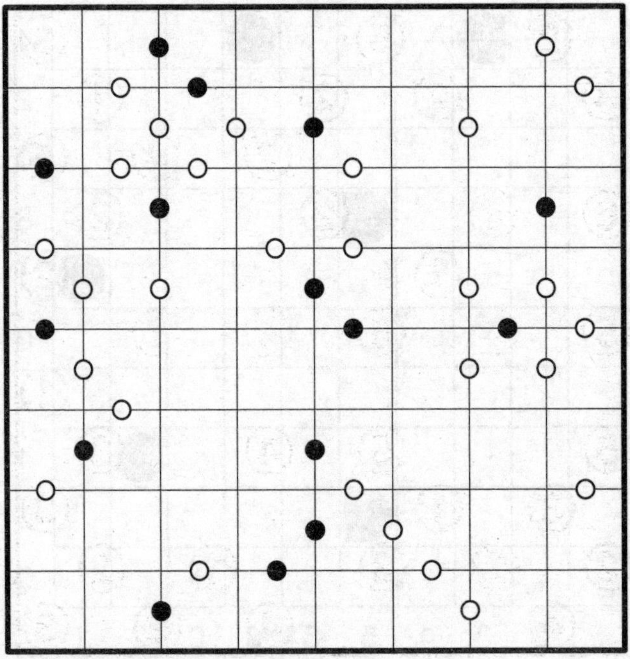

Instructions

Place digits from 1 to 8 once each in every row and column.

- Squares separated by a white dot must contain two consecutive numbers, such as 2 and 3, or 5 and 6.
- Squares separated by a black dot must contain numbers where one is twice the value of the other, such as 2 and 4.
- All possible dots are given – except where both a black and a white dot could be given, in which case only one dot is shown. The absence of a dot is therefore significant.

Your solving time: ____________

▪ Battleships ▪

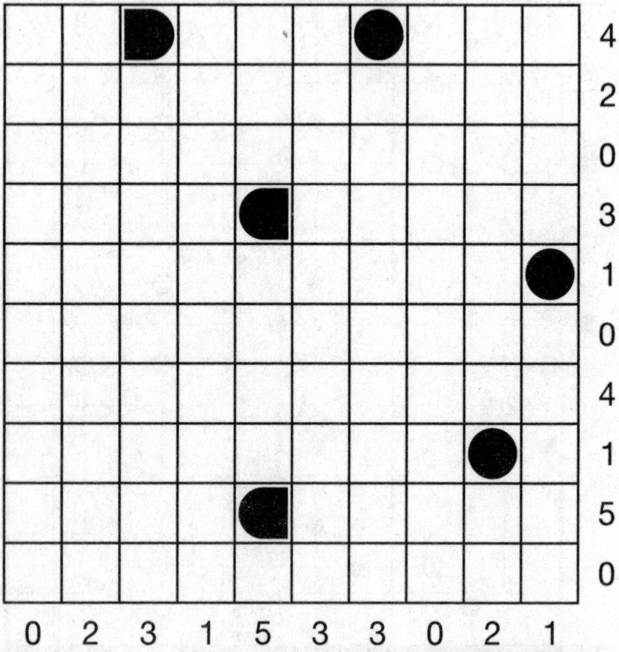

Instructions

Place the given set of 10 ships into the grid.

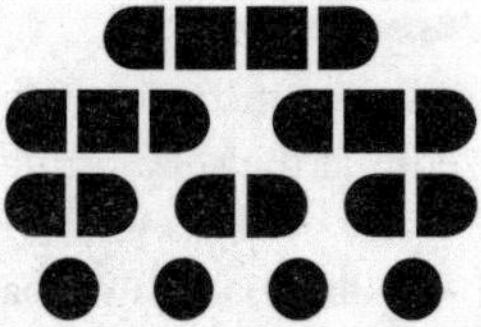

- Clues outside the grid reveal the number of squares in the corresponding row or column that contain a ship part.
- Ships cannot touch each other – not even diagonally.
- Some ship parts are already placed.
- Ships cannot be placed diagonally.

 Your solving time: ____________

▪ Snake ▪

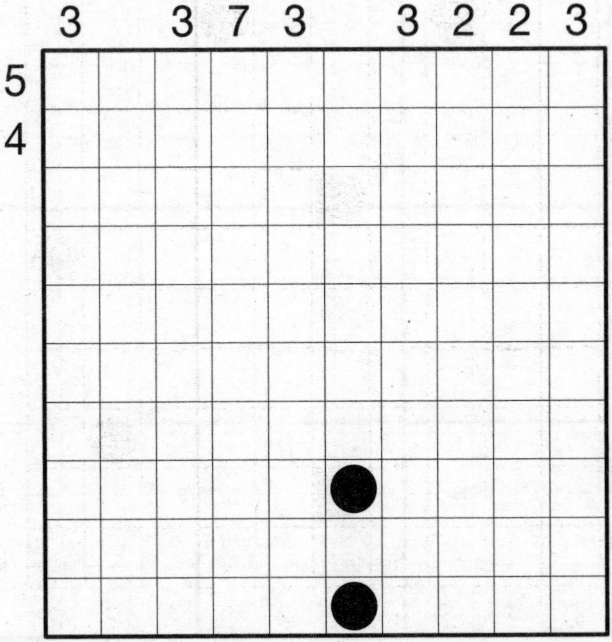

Instructions

Shade some squares to form a single snake that starts and ends at the squares marked with circles.

- A snake is a path of adjacent squares that does not branch or cross over itself.
- The snake does not touch itself – not even diagonally, except when turning a corner.
- Numbers outside the grid reveal the number of squares in their row or column that contain part of the snake.

Your solving time: ____________

▪ Quad Pencil-mark Sudoku ▪

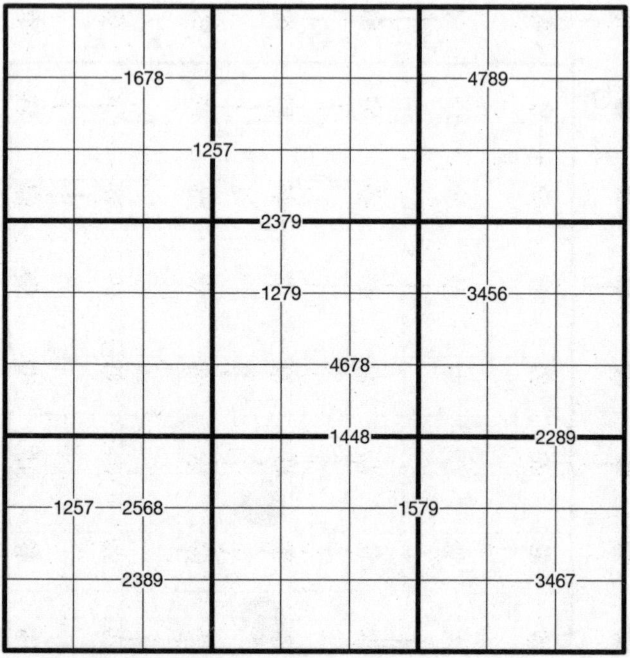

Instructions

Place a digit from 1 to 9 into every square, so that each digit appears once in every row, column and bold-lined 3×3 box.

- Wherever four digits appear on the intersection of four squares, those digits must be placed into those four squares in some order.

Your solving time: ____________

▪ Fences ▪

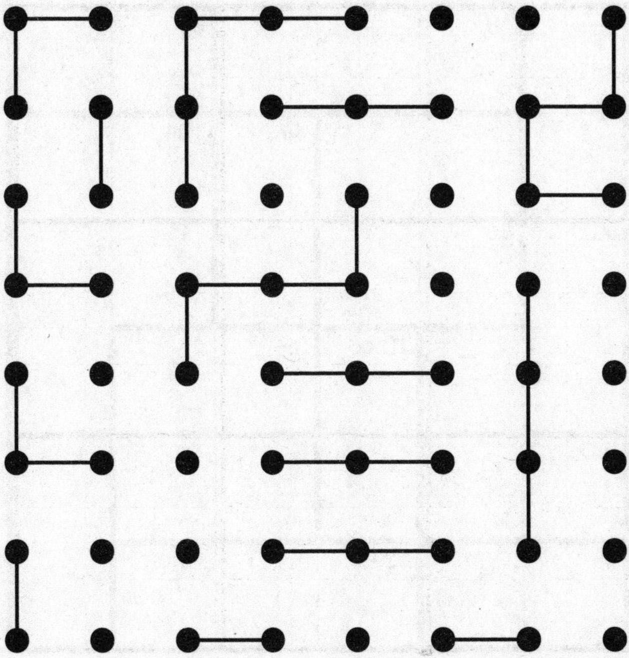

Instructions

Join all of the dots so as to form a single loop.

- The loop does not cross over or touch itself at any point.
- The loop can only consist of horizontal and diagonal lines between dots.

Your solving time: ____________

▪ Calcudoku ▪

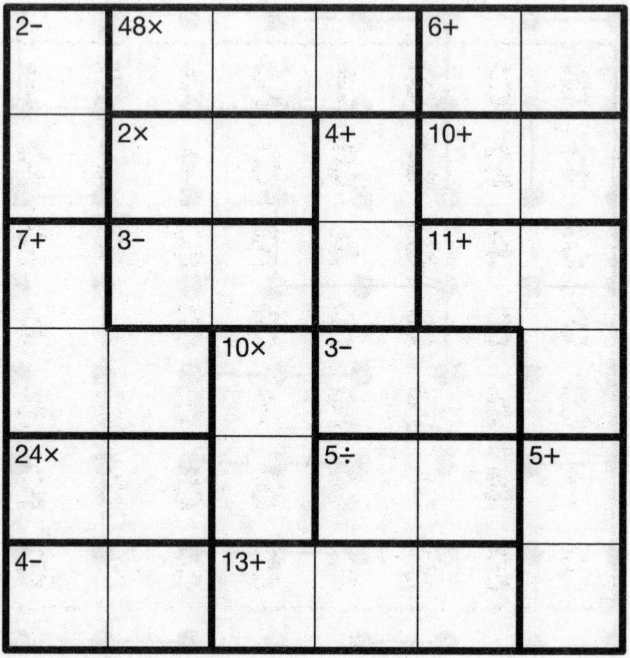

Instructions

Place a digit from 1 to 6 into every square, so that no digit repeats in any row or column.

- The value at the top-left of each bold-lined region must result when all of the numbers in that region have the given operation (+, −, ×, ÷) applied between them. For − and ÷ operations begin with the largest number in the region and then subtract or divide by the other numbers in any order.

Your solving time: ____________

▪ Dominoes ▪

6	0	5	1	2	1	5	1
4	2	3	5	0	1	4	2
3	4	5	4	2	3	0	2
5	0	0	6	6	6	1	4
5	4	2	2	1	6	0	4
1	4	1	3	3	5	5	2
3	3	6	0	6	3	6	0

Instructions

Draw solid lines to divide the grid up to form a complete set of standard dominoes, with exactly one of each domino.

- A '0' represents a blank on a traditional domino.
- Use the check-off chart to help you keep track of which dominoes you've placed.

0	1	2	3	4	5	6	
							0
							1
							2
							3
							4
							5
							6

Your solving time: ____________

▪ King's Journey ▪

							40
30	32		26		38	37	
15			3	1		42	
							43
		17		22			46
6			60			64	
	10				63		49
8			57	56		52	50

Instructions

Write a number in each of the empty squares so that the grid contains every number from 1 to 64 exactly once.

- Place the numbers so that there is a route from 1 to 64 that visits every grid square exactly once in increasing numerical order, moving only left, right, up, down or diagonally between touching squares.

Your solving time: __________

▪ Skyscrapers ▪

	4		1	3		
2						
3						
3						
						2

Instructions

Place a digit from 1 to 5 into every square, so that no digit repeats in any row or column inside the grid.

- Each clue number outside the grid gives the number of digits that are 'visible' from that point, looking along that clue's row or column. A digit is visible unless there is a higher digit preceding it, reading from the clue along the row or column. E.g. the clue to the left of 14235 would be 3, since 1, 4 and 5 are visible, but 2 and 3 are obscured by 4.

Your solving time: ______________

▪ Four in a Row ▪

×		o	o		×	×	
×	×	×		×	×		×
		×		×		o	
		o					×
		×		o	o		
o		o				o	o
o			o	×		×	
	×	o		o	o	×	×

Instructions

Place either an × or an o into every empty square.

- Complete the grid *without* forming any lines of four or more ×s or os.
- Lines can be formed in horizontal, vertical and diagonal directions.

Your solving time: ____________

▪ Slitherlink ▪

3	2	2	3		3	2	3
3	2		2		2	3	2
2		1	1	3		2	2
3	3				1		
		3				3	3
2	2		2	3	2		2
2	1	1		1		2	3
3	3	3		3	2	1	3

Instructions

Draw a single loop by connecting together some, but not necessarily all, dots so that each numbered square has the specified number of adjacent line segments.

- Dots can only be joined by horizontal or vertical lines.
- The loop cannot touch, cross or overlap itself in any way.

Your solving time: ________________

▪ Walls ▪

Instructions

Draw a horizontal or vertical line across the full width or height of the centre of every white square.

- The total length of all lines touching each black square must be equal to the number printed on that cell.
- The length of a line is defined as the number of squares it covers.
- Some lines may be shared between black squares; other lines may not touch any black squares.

Your solving time: ____________

▪ Written Logic ▪

		Position			Speed		
		First	Second	Third	24mph	26mph	28mph
Cyclist	Patel						
	Thomson						
	Walker						
Speed	24mph						
	26mph						
	28mph						

Cyclist	Position	Speed

Cycling Race

Three cyclists – Patel, Thomson and Walker – are racing. At a given moment in the race, one of them is travelling at 24mph, one at 26mph and the third at 28mph. What is the position and speed of each cyclist, given the following facts?

- Patel is going slower than the cyclist in second place.
- The cyclist going at 28mph is ahead of Walker.
- The name of the cyclist in last place is later in the alphabet than the name of the cyclist going at 24mph.

Your solving time: ____________

▪ Path Finder ▪

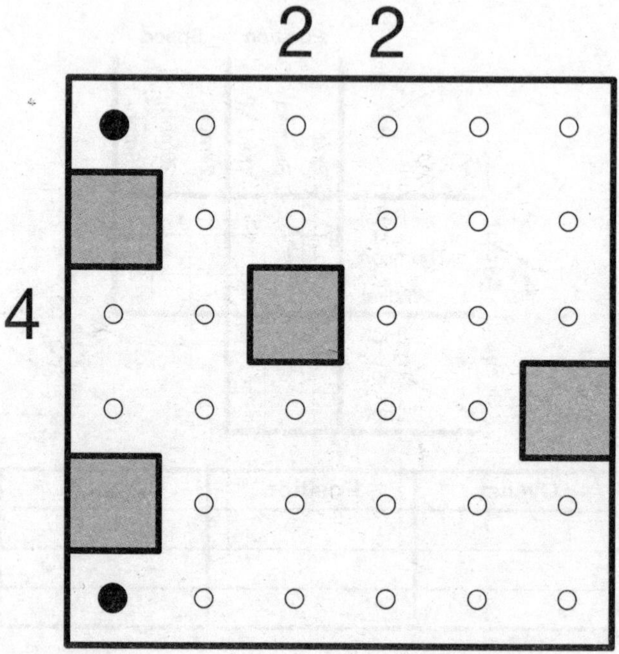

Instructions

Join some of the dots to form a single path which does not touch or cross itself at any point.

- The start and end of the path are indicated by black dots.
- Numbers outside the grid specify the number of dots in their row or column that are visited by the path.
- The path can't touch or cross over any of the shaded boxes.
- The path is constructed only of horizontal and vertical line segments.

Your solving time: ____________

▪ Sudoku 3D Star ▪

Instructions

Place a digit from 1 to 8 into each empty square, so that no digit repeats in any row or column of 8 squares, or any bold-lined 4×2 or 2×4 box.

- Rows and columns start at one edge of the grid and follow along the same row or column until they reach half way across the grid; then they bend with the 3D surface and continue until they reach a different edge of the grid.

Your solving time: ____________

▪ Loop Finder ▪

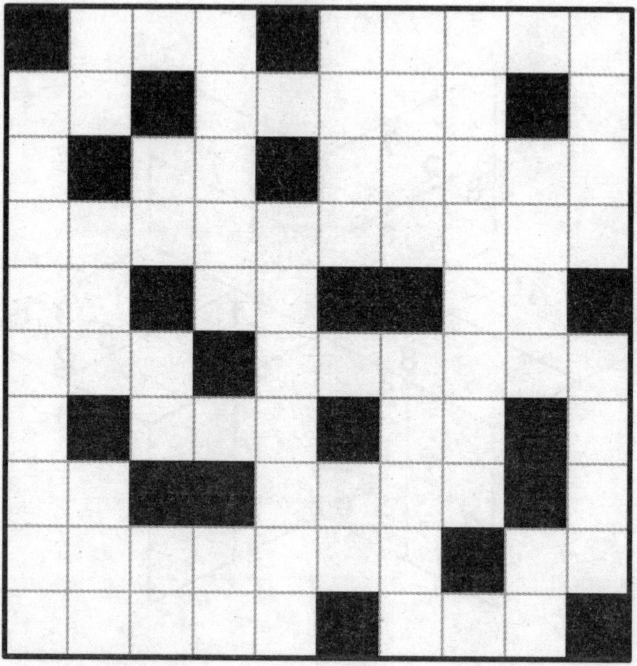

Instructions

Draw a single loop which visits every white square exactly once.

- The loop cannot touch or cross over either itself or a black square at any point.
- The loop consists only of horizontal and vertical line segments.

Your solving time: ____________

▪ Touchy ▪

	F					E	
H							B
			H	A			
	H	C			B	F	
	E	G			A	H	
			E	G			
F							G
	A					D	

Instructions

Place a letter from A to H into every square, so that no letter repeats in any row or column.

- Identical letters cannot be in diagonally touching squares.

Your solving time: ______________

▪ Frame Sudoku ▪

	6	10	5	3	9	9	
13							8
8							13
8							13
13							8
8							13
13							8
	6	8	7	10	5	6	

Instructions

Place a digit from 1 to 6 into every square, so that no digit repeats in any row or column.

- Clue numbers outside the grid give the sum of all the digits that are in the adjacent 3×2 box *and* that are in the same row or column as the clue.

Your solving time: ____________

▪ Binary Placement ▪

0		1		0			
		1	0		0	1	
			0				0
1						1	
	1						1
0				1			
	1	0		1	1		
			1		1		0

Instructions

Place 0 or 1 in every empty square so that there are an equal number of each digit in every row and column.

- Reading along any row or column, there must not be more than two of the same digit in direct succession. For example, 10011001 would be a valid row, while 10001101 would not be valid due to the three 0s in direct succession.

Your solving time: ____________

▪ Hanjie ▪

	4	4	4	4	4	10	8	6	4	2
1										
2										
3										
9										
10										
10										
9										
3										
2										
1										

Clue: Look right

Instructions

Shade some squares while obeying the clues at the start of each row or column.

- The clues provide, in reading order, the length of every run of consecutive shaded squares in each row and column.
- There must be a gap of at least one empty square between each run of shaded squares in the same row or column.
- The finished puzzle will reveal a simple picture which fits the clue given beneath.

Your solving time: ____________

▪ Number Link ▪

		1							
1				2		3	4		
		2							
5			6				5		
		7			8				
							4	9	
	8						10		
		7							
10	6			9					
			3						

Instructions

Draw a set of separate paths, with one path connecting each pair of identical numbers.

- No more than one path can enter any square, and paths can only travel horizontally or vertically between squares.
- Paths cannot touch or cross one another.

Your solving time: ______________

▪ Kakuro ▪

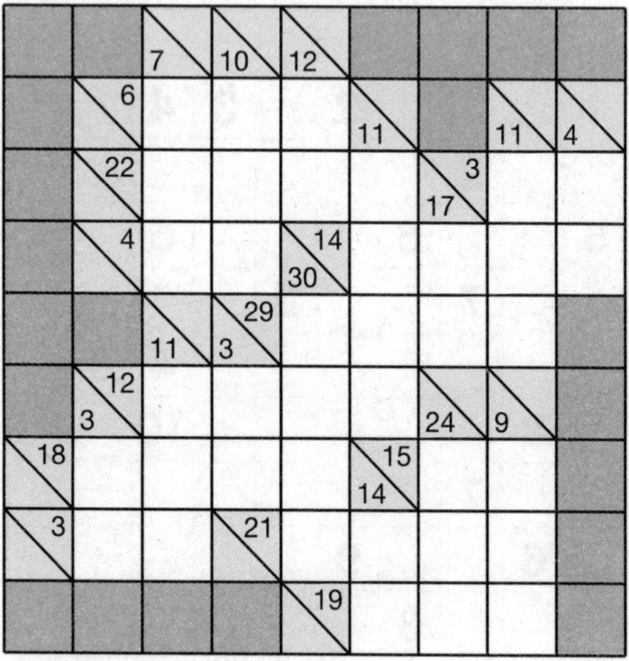

Instructions

Place a digit from 1 to 9 into each white square, and so that no placed digit repeats in any consecutive horizontal or vertical 'run' of squares.

- Each horizontal or vertical 'run' has a total given immediately to its left or above respectively. The digits in that run must add up to the given total.

 Your solving time: ___________

▪ Arrow Sudoku ▪

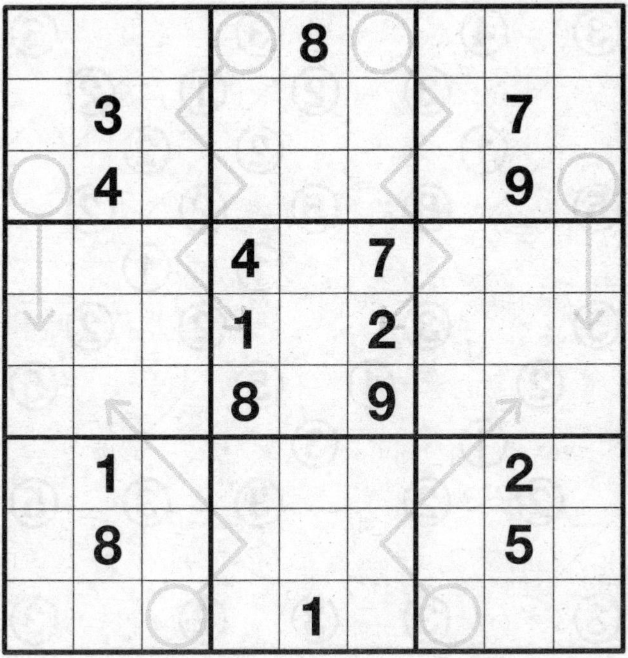

				8				
	3						7	
	4						9	
			4		7			
			1		2			
			8		9			
	1						2	
	8						5	
				1				

Instructions

Place a digit from 1 to 9 into every empty square, so that each digit appears once in every row, column and bold-lined 3×3 box.

- Circled squares must contain a value equal to the sum of the digits along their attached arrows.

Your solving time: ____________

▪ Bridges ▪

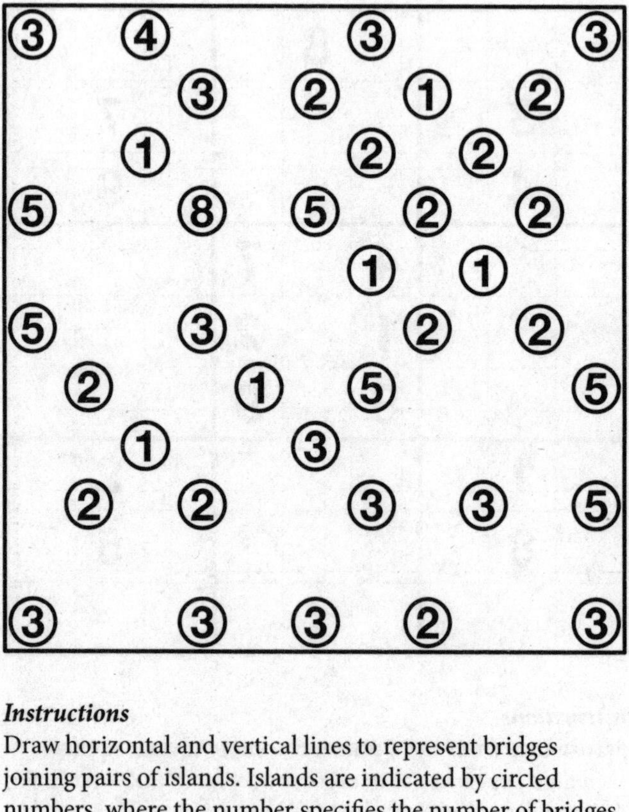

Instructions

Draw horizontal and vertical lines to represent bridges joining pairs of islands. Islands are indicated by circled numbers, where the number specifies the number of bridges that connect to that island.

- Any pair of islands may be joined by up to two bridges.
- Bridges may not cross either another bridge or an island.
- All islands must be joined together by the bridges, so you can travel to any island just by following the bridges.

Your solving time: ____________

▪ Kropki ▪

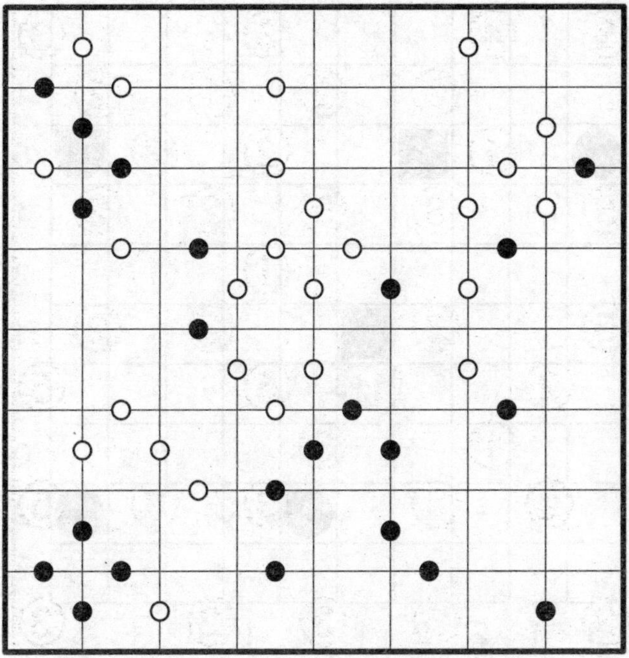

Instructions

Place digits from 1 to 8 once each in every row and column.

- Squares separated by a white dot must contain two consecutive numbers, such as 2 and 3, or 5 and 6.
- Squares separated by a black dot must contain numbers where one is twice the value of the other, such as 2 and 4.
- All possible dots are given – except where both a black and a white dot could be given, in which case only one dot is shown. The absence of a dot is therefore significant.

Your solving time: ____________

▪ Battleships ▪

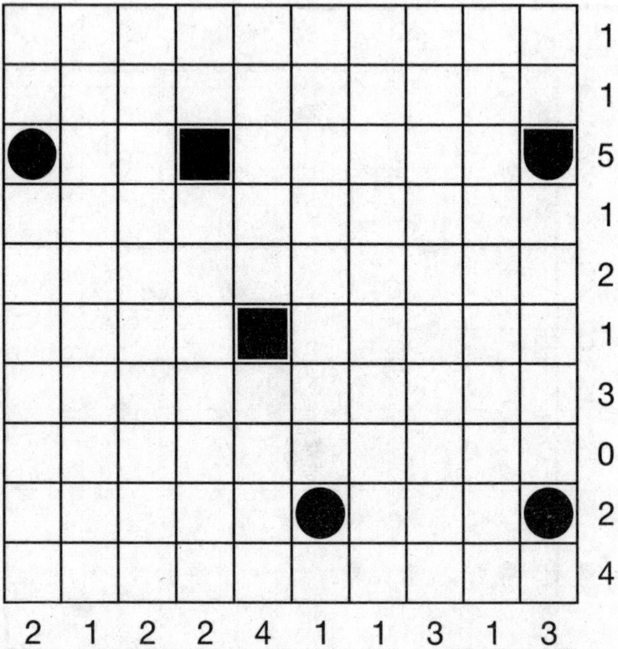

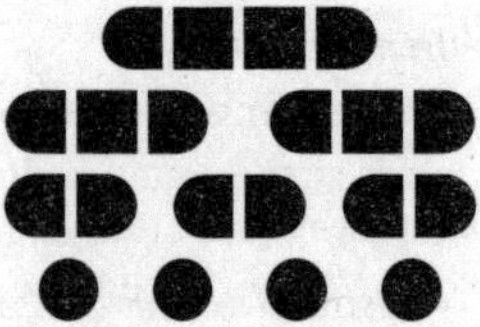

Instructions

Place the given set of 10 ships into the grid.

- Clues outside the grid reveal the number of squares in the corresponding row or column that contain a ship part.
- Ships cannot touch each other – not even diagonally.
- Some ship parts are already placed.
- Ships cannot be placed diagonally.

Your solving time: ____________

▪ Snake ▪

	3		6	4	6	3		5	4	
2					●					
3										
6										
3										
4										
4					●					

Instructions

Shade some squares to form a single snake that starts and ends at the squares marked with circles.

- A snake is a path of adjacent squares that does not branch or cross over itself.
- The snake does not touch itself – not even diagonally, except when turning a corner.
- Numbers outside the grid reveal the number of squares in their row or column that contain part of the snake.

Your solving time: ______________

▪ Quad Pencil-mark Sudoku ▪

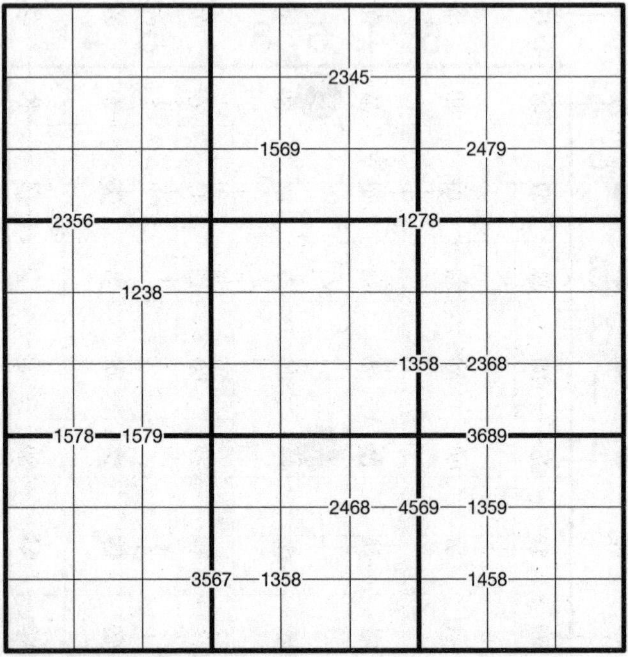

Instructions

Place a digit from 1 to 9 into every square, so that each digit appears once in every row, column and bold-lined 3×3 box.

- Wherever four digits appear on the intersection of four squares, those digits must be placed into those four squares in some order.

Your solving time: ___________

▪ Fences ▪

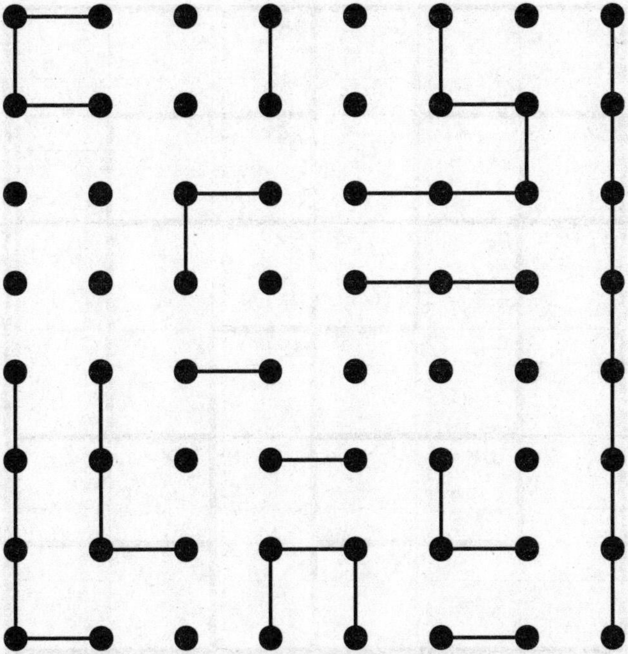

Instructions

Join all of the dots so as to form a single loop.

- The loop does not cross over or touch itself at any point.
- The loop can only consist of horizontal and diagonal lines between dots.

Your solving time: ____________

▪ Calcudoku ▪

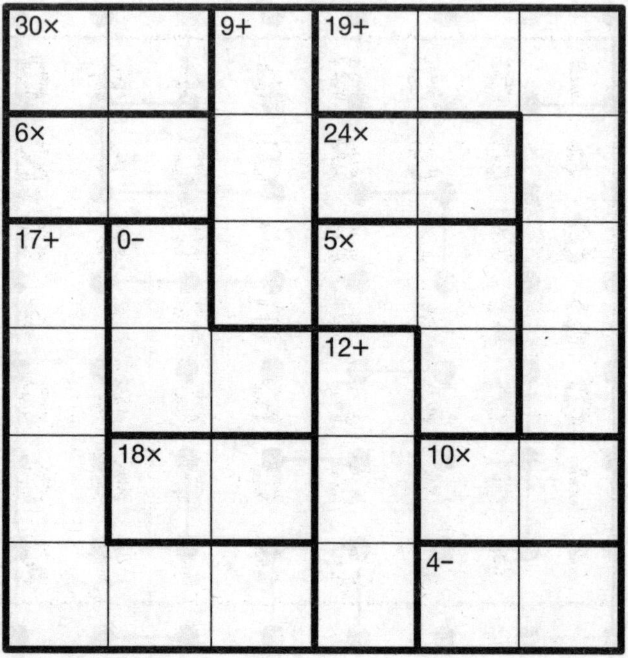

Instructions

Place a digit from 1 to 6 into every square, so that no digit repeats in any row or column.

- The value at the top-left of each bold-lined region must result when all of the numbers in that region have the given operation (+, –, ×, ÷) applied between them. For – and ÷ operations begin with the largest number in the region and then subtract or divide by the other numbers in any order.

 Your solving time: ____________

▪ Dominoes ▪

1	6	0	5	4	4	4	0
4	3	3	6	6	0	4	2
3	1	1	2	1	5	5	6
3	2	6	6	5	2	1	4
0	5	3	2	2	0	5	0
1	5	4	3	0	6	6	0
1	4	2	3	3	1	5	2

Instructions

Draw solid lines to divide the grid up to form a complete set of standard dominoes, with exactly one of each domino.

- A '0' represents a blank on a traditional domino.
- Use the check-off chart to help you keep track of which dominoes you've placed.

0	1	2	3	4	5	6	
							0
							1
							2
							3
							4
							5
							6

Your solving time: ____________

▪ King's Journey ▪

64		57					45
63	61	58			49		
				55		43	
	5		1		33	42	
		2			35	36	
	8		28				38
	14	17	18	27	26		23
		16				25	

Instructions

Write a number in each of the empty squares so that the grid contains every number from 1 to 64 exactly once.

- Place the numbers so that there is a route from 1 to 64 that visits every grid square exactly once in increasing numerical order, moving only left, right, up, down or diagonally between touching squares.

Your solving time: ___________

▪ Skyscrapers ▪

			4			
4						
4						
						2
		1			3	

Instructions

Place a digit from 1 to 5 into every square, so that no digit repeats in any row or column inside the grid.

- Each clue number outside the grid gives the number of digits that are 'visible' from that point, looking along that clue's row or column. A digit is visible unless there is a higher digit preceding it, reading from the clue along the row or column. E.g. the clue to the left of 14235 would be 3, since 1, 4 and 5 are visible, but 2 and 3 are obscured by 4.

Your solving time: ____________

▪ Four in a Row ▪

O	X	X	O		X	X	O
				X	X		
O		X			X		
O			O			O	O
	X	O			X		O
		O	O			X	
	O		X		X		
X			O	O			X

Instructions

Place either an × or an o into every empty square.

- Complete the grid *without* forming any lines of four or more ×s or os.
- Lines can be formed in horizontal, vertical and diagonal directions.

Your solving time: ____________

▪ Slitherlink ▪

3	2			3	2	1	3
3		2				2	3
3	0	1	2	3	2		3
3		3		1		1	3
3	1		2		3		2
2		3	2	3	1	3	2
2	2				1		1
3	2	1	0			2	3

Instructions

Draw a single loop by connecting together some, but not necessarily all, dots so that each numbered square has the specified number of adjacent line segments.

- Dots can only be joined by horizontal or vertical lines.
- The loop cannot touch, cross or overlap itself in any way.

Your solving time: ____________

▪ Walls ▪

Instructions

Draw a horizontal or vertical line across the full width or height of the centre of every white square.

- The total length of all lines touching each black square must be equal to the number printed on that cell.
- The length of a line is defined as the number of squares it covers.
- Some lines may be shared between black squares; other lines may not touch any black squares.

Your solving time: ____________

▪ Written Logic ▪

		Quantity			Price		
		3	4	6	20p	30p	50p
Fruit	Apples						
	Bananas						
	Oranges						
Price	20p						
	30p						
	50p						

Fruit	Quantity	Price

Fruit Salad

You buy some apples, bananas and oranges, buying three of one, four of another, and six of the third. One costs 20p per fruit, one costs 30p per fruit, and one costs 50p per fruit. How many of each fruit did you buy, at what costs per unit?

- You buy more apples than the 50p fruit.
- The fruit you buy four of is cheaper per fruit than bananas.
- Apples do not cost 20p.
- You buy the most of the cheapest fruit.

Your solving time: ______________

▪ Path Finder ▪

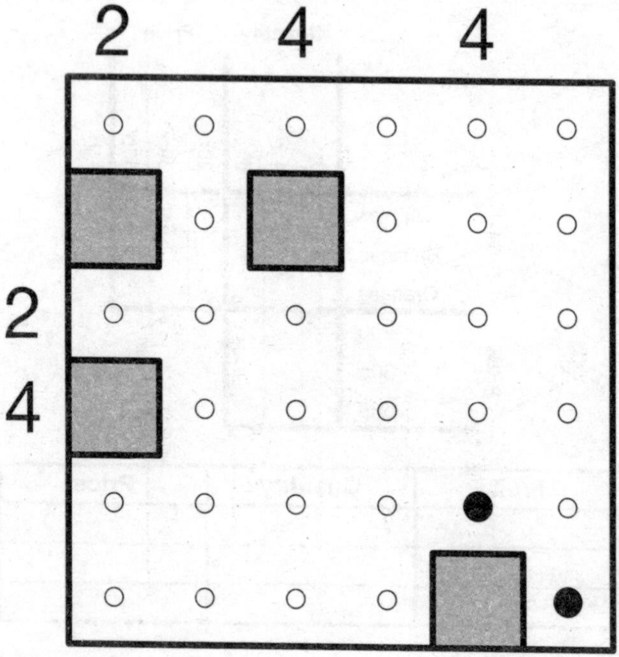

Instructions

Join some of the dots to form a single path which does not touch or cross itself at any point.

- The start and end of the path are indicated by black dots.
- Numbers outside the grid specify the number of dots in their row or column that are visited by the path.
- The path can't touch or cross over any of the shaded boxes.
- The path is constructed only of horizontal and vertical line segments.

Your solving time: ____________

▪ Sudoku 3D Star ▪

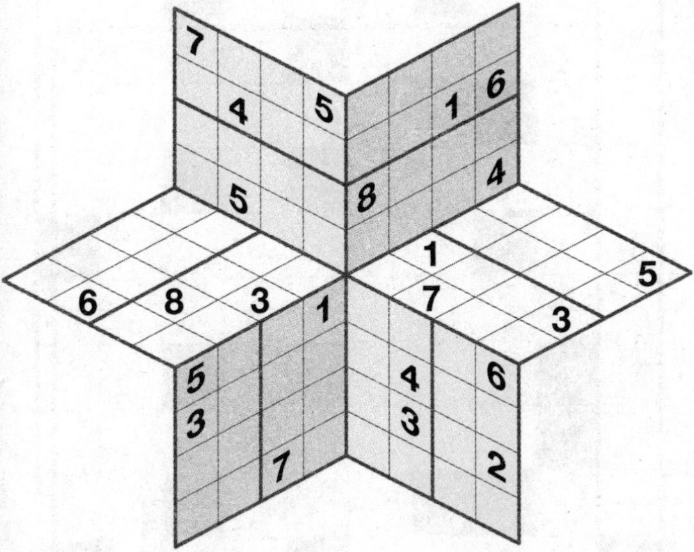

Instructions

Place a digit from 1 to 8 into each empty square, so that no digit repeats in any row or column of 8 squares, or any bold-lined 4×2 or 2×4 box.

- Rows and columns start at one edge of the grid and follow along the same row or column until they reach half way across the grid; then they bend with the 3D surface and continue until they reach a different edge of the grid.

Your solving time: ____________

▪ Loop Finder ▪

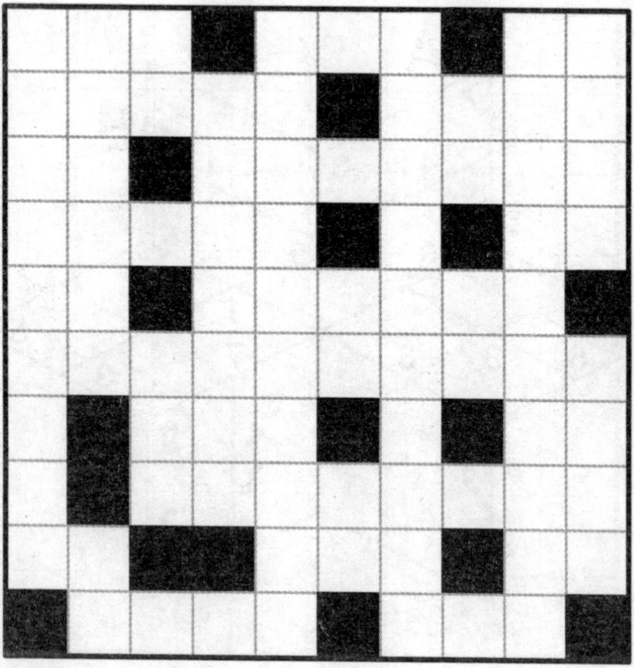

Instructions

Draw a single loop which visits every white square exactly once.

- The loop cannot touch or cross over either itself or a black square at any point.
- The loop consists only of horizontal and vertical line segments.

Your solving time: ____________

▪ Touchy ▪

		A			F		
	E					B	
	H					F	
B		E			G		H
G		F			C		E
	A					G	
	F					H	
		G			D		

Instructions

Place a letter from A to H into every square, so that no letter repeats in any row or column.

- Identical letters cannot be in diagonally touching squares.

Your solving time: ____________

▪ Frame Sudoku ▪

	5	10	6	3	10	8	
8							13
13							8
6							15
15							6
13							8
8							13
	9	4	8	11	5	5	

Instructions

Place a digit from 1 to 6 into every square, so that no digit repeats in any row or column.

- Clue numbers outside the grid give the sum of all the digits that are in the adjacent 3×2 box *and* that are in the same row or column as the clue.

Your solving time: ____________

▪ Binary Placement ▪

0	1		0		0		
0				1	0		
	0						
0				1	0		1
1		1	1				0
						1	
		0	1				0
		0		0		0	0

Instructions

Place 0 or 1 in every empty square so that there are an equal number of each digit in every row and column.

- Reading along any row or column, there must not be more than two of the same digit in direct succession. For example, 10011001 would be a valid row, while 10001101 would not be valid due to the three 0s in direct succession.

Your solving time: ______________

▪ Hanjie ▪

	6	2, 2	2, 2, 2	1, 2, 2, 1	1, 1, 1	1, 1, 1	1, 2, 2, 1	2, 2, 2	2, 2	6
6										
2, 2										
2, 2										
1, 2, 2, 1										
1, 2, 2, 1										
1, 1										
1, 1, 1, 1										
2, 4, 2										
2, 2										
6										

Clue: Feeling happy

Instructions

Shade some squares while obeying the clues at the start of each row or column.

- The clues provide, in reading order, the length of every run of consecutive shaded squares in each row and column.
- There must be a gap of at least one empty square between each run of shaded squares in the same row or column.
- The finished puzzle will reveal a simple picture which fits the clue given beneath.

Your solving time: ______________

▪ Number Link ▪

1							2		
		3			4			5	
				5					
	4		3				6	7	
	6		2		7				
	1								
								8	
9	8	9							

Instructions

Draw a set of separate paths, with one path connecting each pair of identical numbers.

- No more than one path can enter any square, and paths can only travel horizontally or vertically between squares.
- Paths cannot touch or cross one another.

Your solving time: ______________

▪ Kakuro ▪

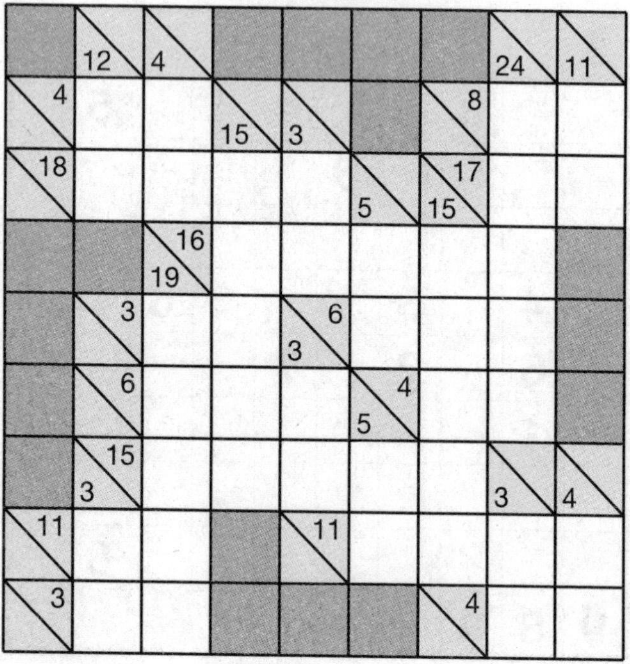

Instructions

Place a digit from 1 to 9 into each white square, and so that no placed digit repeats in any consecutive horizontal or vertical 'run' of squares.

- Each horizontal or vertical 'run' has a total given immediately to its left or above respectively. The digits in that run must add up to the given total.

 Your solving time: ____________

▪ Arrow Sudoku ▪

3		7		5		4		1
	9						3	
	4						8	
		8				9		
	3						1	
	7						9	
9		2		6		3		4

Instructions

Place a digit from 1 to 9 into every empty square, so that each digit appears once in every row, column and bold-lined 3×3 box.

- Circled squares must contain a value equal to the sum of the digits along their attached arrows.

Your solving time: ____________

▪ Bridges ▪

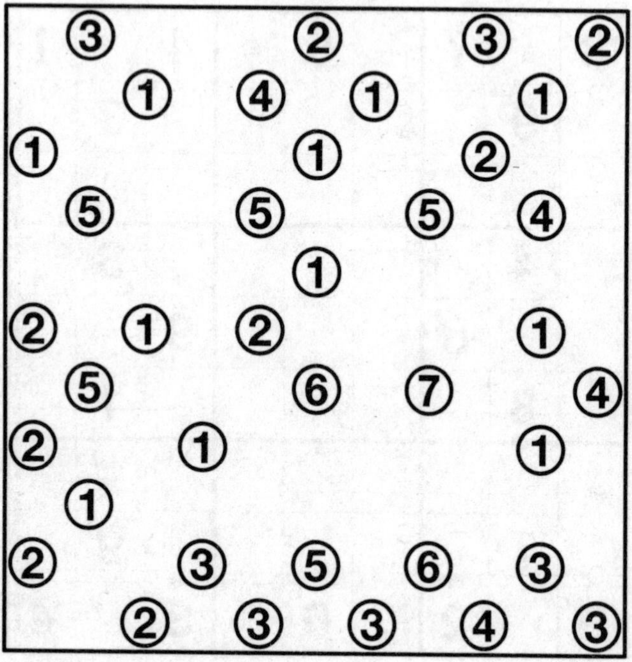

Instructions

Draw horizontal and vertical lines to represent bridges joining pairs of islands. Islands are indicated by circled numbers, where the number specifies the number of bridges that connect to that island.

- Any pair of islands may be joined by up to two bridges.
- Bridges may not cross either another bridge or an island.
- All islands must be joined together by the bridges, so you can travel to any island just by following the bridges.

Your solving time: ____________

▪ Kropki ▪

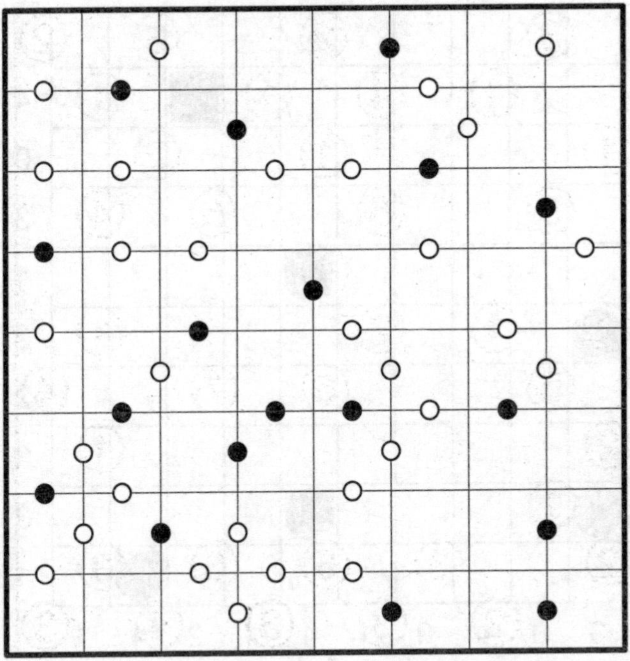

Instructions

Place digits from 1 to 8 once each in every row and column.

- Squares separated by a white dot must contain two consecutive numbers, such as 2 and 3, or 5 and 6.
- Squares separated by a black dot must contain numbers where one is twice the value of the other, such as 2 and 4.
- All possible dots are given – except where both a black and a white dot could be given, in which case only one dot is shown. The absence of a dot is therefore significant.

Your solving time: ______________

▪ Battleships ▪

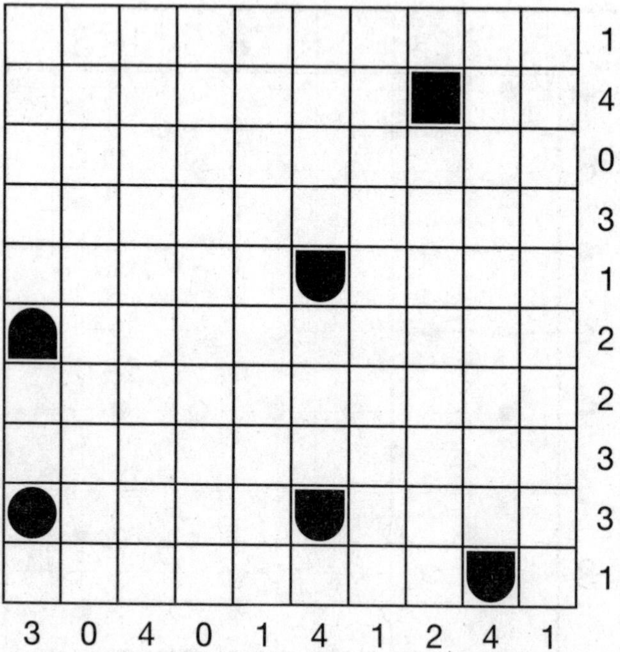

Instructions

Place the given set of 10 ships into the grid.

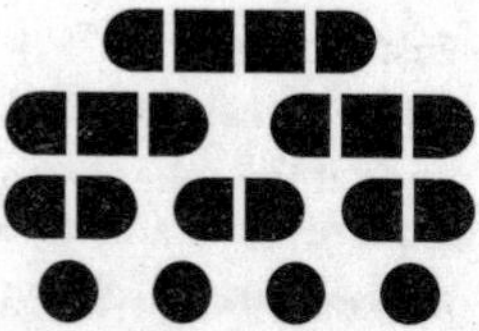

- Clues outside the grid reveal the number of squares in the corresponding row or column that contain a ship part.
- Ships cannot touch each other – not even diagonally.
- Some ship parts are already placed.
- Ships cannot be placed diagonally.

Your solving time: ____________

▪ Snake ▪

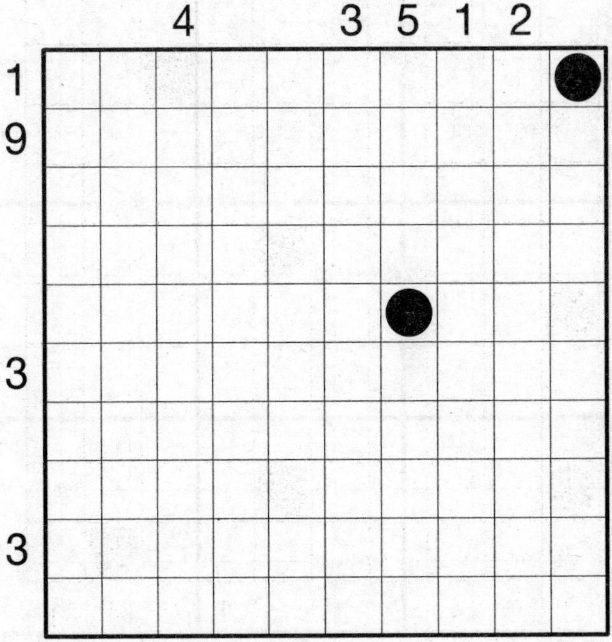

Instructions

Shade some squares to form a single snake that starts and ends at the squares marked with circles.

- A snake is a path of adjacent squares that does not branch or cross over itself.
- The snake does not touch itself – not even diagonally, except when turning a corner.
- Numbers outside the grid reveal the number of squares in their row or column that contain part of the snake.

Your solving time: ______________

▪ Quad Pencil-mark Sudoku ▪

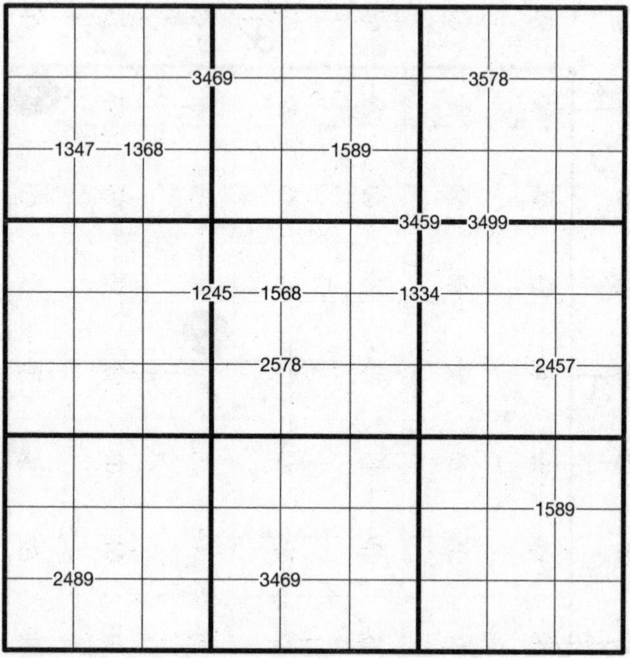

Instructions

Place a digit from 1 to 9 into every square, so that each digit appears once in every row, column and bold-lined 3×3 box.

- Wherever four digits appear on the intersection of four squares, those digits must be placed into those four squares in some order.

 Your solving time: ____________

▪ Fences ▪

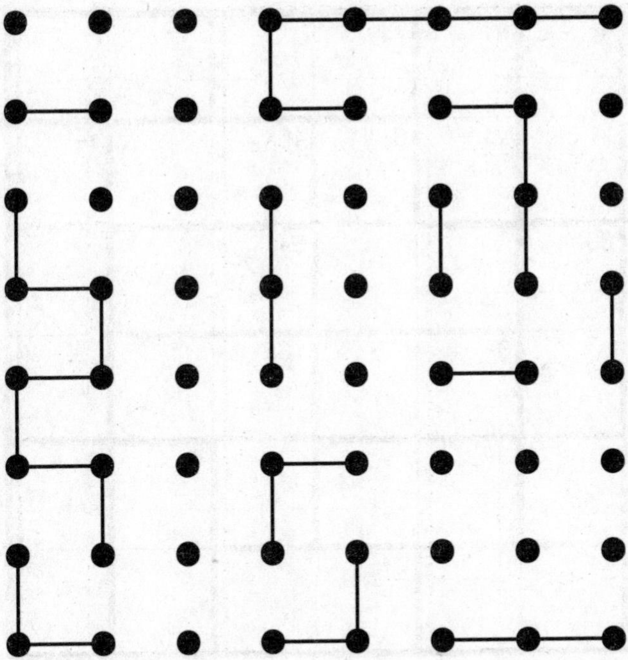

Instructions

Join all of the dots so as to form a single loop.

- The loop does not cross over or touch itself at any point.
- The loop can only consist of horizontal and diagonal lines between dots.

Your solving time: ____________

▪ Calcudoku ▪

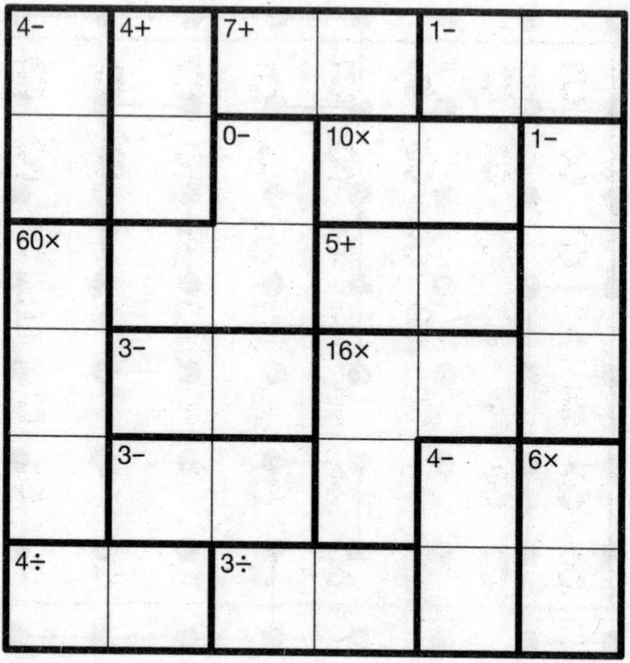

Instructions

Place a digit from 1 to 6 into every square, so that no digit repeats in any row or column.

- The value at the top-left of each bold-lined region must result when all of the numbers in that region have the given operation (+, –, ×, ÷) applied between them. For – and ÷ operations begin with the largest number in the region and then subtract or divide by the other numbers in any order.

Your solving time: ____________

▪ Dominoes ▪

5	0	4	5	5	0	0	0
3	3	3	2	1	2	6	2
6	0	3	4	6	4	1	5
2	2	6	4	0	0	1	5
4	1	5	1	4	2	1	5
3	3	1	4	6	2	1	3
3	0	6	2	6	6	5	4

Instructions

Draw solid lines to divide the grid up to form a complete set of standard dominoes, with exactly one of each domino.

- A '0' represents a blank on a traditional domino.
- Use the check-off chart to help you keep track of which dominoes you've placed.

0	1	2	3	4	5	6	
							0
							1
							2
							3
							4
							5
							6

Your solving time: ____________

▪ King's Journey ▪

27							
		16	17				9
50	25				7		
				22	20	6	
		48				1	
	47		33		58	59	
	43		37		63	62	
	40					64	

Instructions

Write a number in each of the empty squares so that the grid contains every number from 1 to 64 exactly once.

- Place the numbers so that there is a route from 1 to 64 that visits every grid square exactly once in increasing numerical order, moving only left, right, up, down or diagonally between touching squares.

Your solving time: __________

▪ Skyscrapers ▪

				4	4	
1						
						3
4						
						1
	3	2				

Instructions

Place a digit from 1 to 5 into every square, so that no digit repeats in any row or column inside the grid.

- Each clue number outside the grid gives the number of digits that are 'visible' from that point, looking along that clue's row or column. A digit is visible unless there is a higher digit preceding it, reading from the clue along the row or column. E.g. the clue to the left of 14235 would be 3, since 1, 4 and 5 are visible, but 2 and 3 are obscured by 4.

Your solving time: ____________

▪ Four in a Row ▪

O	O			X	X		
O	X	O					
O		O			X	X	
	O		O		X	X	O
O	O					O	
O		O	O	X			
X	X					X	O
X	O	O	X		X	X	

Instructions

Place either an × or an o into every empty square.

- Complete the grid *without* forming any lines of four or more ×s or os.
- Lines can be formed in horizontal, vertical and diagonal directions.

Your solving time: ____________

▪ Slitherlink ▪

	3		3	2	2		3
3	1	2	2	3		1	2
	2		1		0	2	2
1		3		3		3	1
3	2		2		1		3
2	3	2		1		2	
1	2		2	1	3	2	0
3		2	3	1		0	

Instructions

Draw a single loop by connecting together some, but not necessarily all, dots so that each numbered square has the specified number of adjacent line segments.

- Dots can only be joined by horizontal or vertical lines.
- The loop cannot touch, cross or overlap itself in any way.

Your solving time: ____________

▪ Walls ▪

4		2			4		
	2					2	
		4					
				6			6
5			5				
					3		
	5					2	
		4			4		4

Instructions

Draw a horizontal or vertical line across the full width or height of the centre of every white square.

- The total length of all lines touching each black square must be equal to the number printed on that cell.
- The length of a line is defined as the number of squares it covers.
- Some lines may be shared between black squares; other lines may not touch any black squares.

Your solving time: ______________

▪ Written Logic ▪

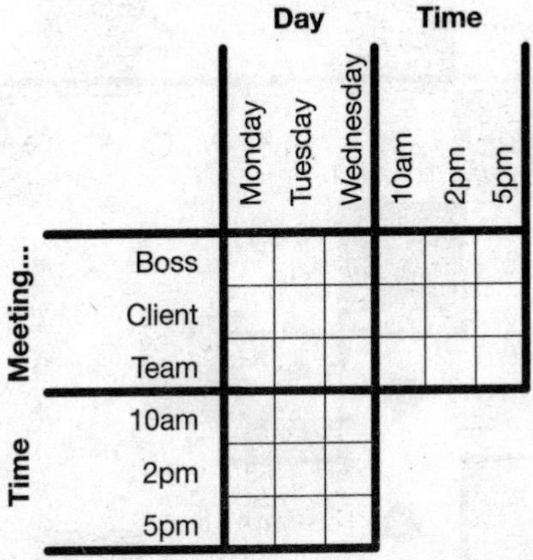

Meeting...	Day	Time

Meeting Mix-up

You have three meetings scheduled this week: with your boss, with a client and with your team. The meetings are on Monday, Tuesday and Wednesday. They are at 10am, 2pm and 5pm. At what time and date will each meeting occur?

- Your 10am meeting is the day after your team meeting.
- Your Tuesday meeting is later in the day than your meeting with your boss.
- Your client meeting is later in the day than the team one.

Your solving time: ____________

▪ Path Finder ▪

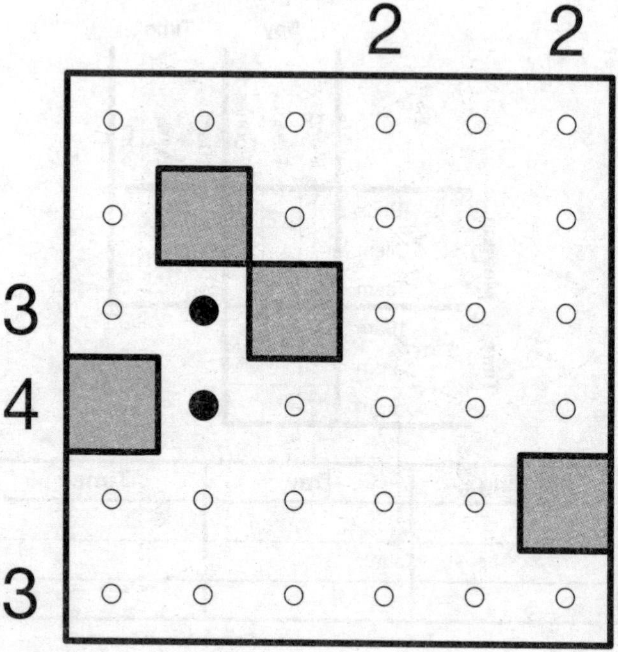

Instructions

Join some of the dots to form a single path which does not touch or cross itself at any point.

- The start and end of the path are indicated by black dots.
- Numbers outside the grid specify the number of dots in their row or column that are visited by the path.
- The path can't touch or cross over any of the shaded boxes.
- The path is constructed only of horizontal and vertical line segments.

 Your solving time: ____________

▪ Sudoku 3D Star ▪

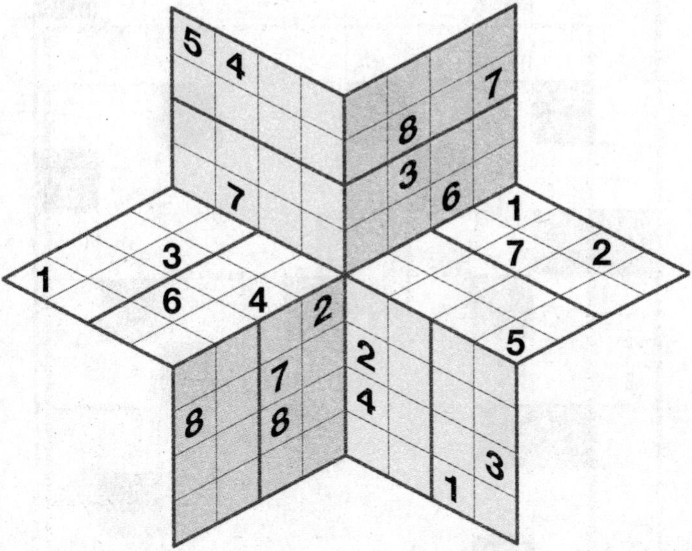

Instructions

Place a digit from 1 to 8 into each empty square, so that no digit repeats in any row or column of 8 squares, or any bold-lined 4×2 or 2×4 box.

- Rows and columns start at one edge of the grid and follow along the same row or column until they reach half way across the grid; then they bend with the 3D surface and continue until they reach a different edge of the grid.

Your solving time: ____________

▪ Loop Finder ▪

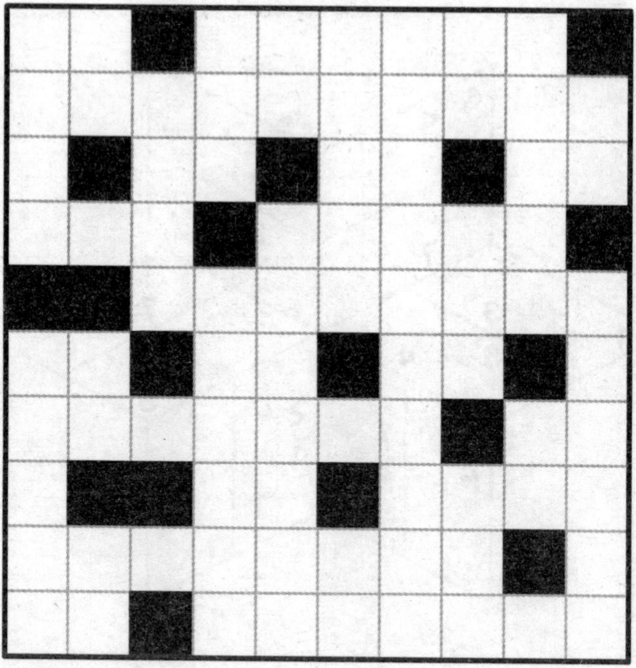

Instructions

Draw a single loop which visits every white square exactly once.

- The loop cannot touch or cross over either itself or a black square at any point.
- The loop consists only of horizontal and vertical line segments.

Your solving time: ____________

▪ Touchy ▪

		B	D	G	H		
C	E					H	F
A							C
B							D
G	C					F	B
		G	F	A	C		

Instructions

Place a letter from A to H into every square, so that no letter repeats in any row or column.

- Identical letters cannot be in diagonally touching squares.

Your solving time: ______________

▪ Frame Sudoku ▪

	4	8	9	4	8	9	
14							7
7							14
7							14
14							7
7							14
14							7
	8	9	4	8	9	4	

Instructions

Place a digit from 1 to 6 into every square, so that no digit repeats in any row or column.

- Clue numbers outside the grid give the sum of all the digits that are in the adjacent 3×2 box *and* that are in the same row or column as the clue.

Your solving time: ______________

▪ Binary Placement ▪

1					1		
	0	1		1		1	
	1	0		1			0
	0			0			
			0			0	
0			0		0	1	
	0		1		1	1	
		0					0

Instructions

Place 0 or 1 in every empty square so that there are an equal number of each digit in every row and column.

- Reading along any row or column, there must not be more than two of the same digit in direct succession. For example, 10011001 would be a valid row, while 10001101 would not be valid due to the three 0s in direct succession.

Your solving time: ____________

▪ Hanjie ▪

							1	1	1	
					1	1	1	1	1	
	2	4	4	8	1	1	2	4	4	8
4										
3, 1										
1, 4										
3, 1										
1, 1										
1, 3										
3, 4										
4, 4										
4, 2										
2										

Clue: Tuneful

Instructions

Shade some squares while obeying the clues at the start of each row or column.

- The clues provide, in reading order, the length of every run of consecutive shaded squares in each row and column.
- There must be a gap of at least one empty square between each run of shaded squares in the same row or column.
- The finished puzzle will reveal a simple picture which fits the clue given beneath.

 Your solving time: ____________

▪ Number Link ▪

					1				
	2	3		4			3	5	
						6			
	7		8		9				1
					10				6
		8							
			2						
		7		4	10			5	
				9					

Instructions

Draw a set of separate paths, with one path connecting each pair of identical numbers.

- No more than one path can enter any square, and paths can only travel horizontally or vertically between squares.
- Paths cannot touch or cross one another.

Your solving time: ______________

▪ Kakuro ▪

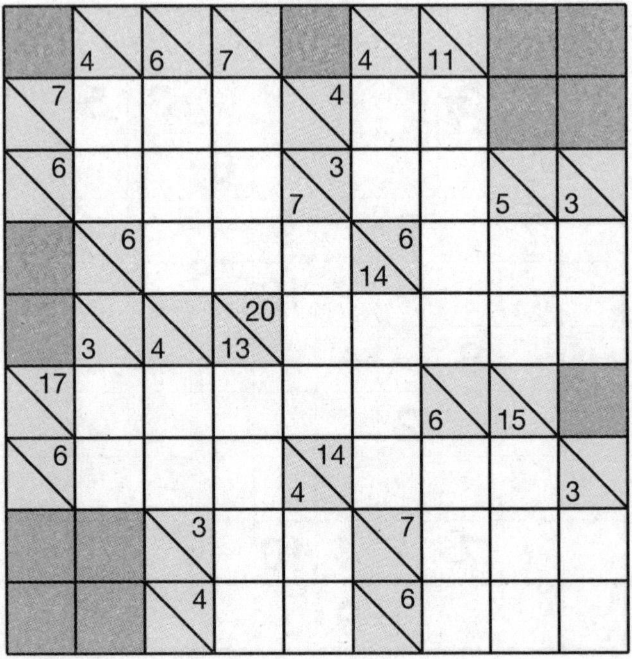

Instructions

Place a digit from 1 to 9 into each white square, and so that no placed digit repeats in any consecutive horizontal or vertical 'run' of squares.

- Each horizontal or vertical 'run' has a total given immediately to its left or above respectively. The digits in that run must add up to the given total.

 Your solving time: ___________

▪ Arrow Sudoku ▪

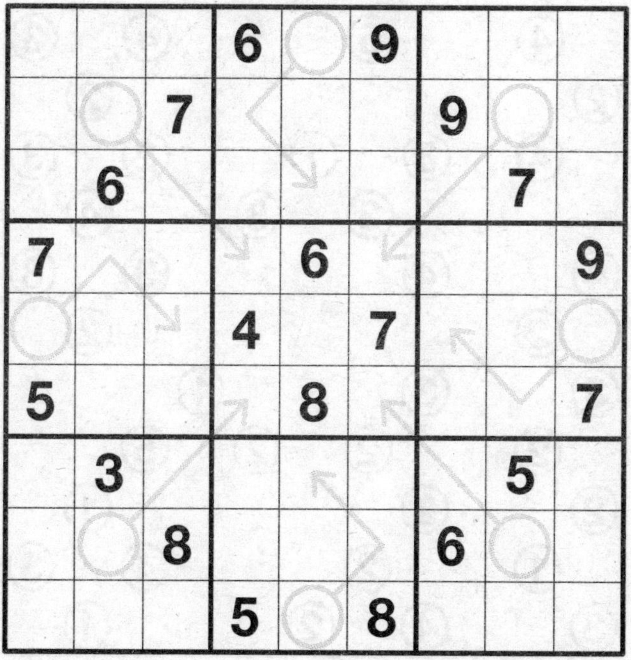

Instructions

Place a digit from 1 to 9 into every empty square, so that each digit appears once in every row, column and bold-lined 3×3 box.

- Circled squares must contain a value equal to the sum of the digits along their attached arrows.

Your solving time: ____________

▪ Bridges ▪

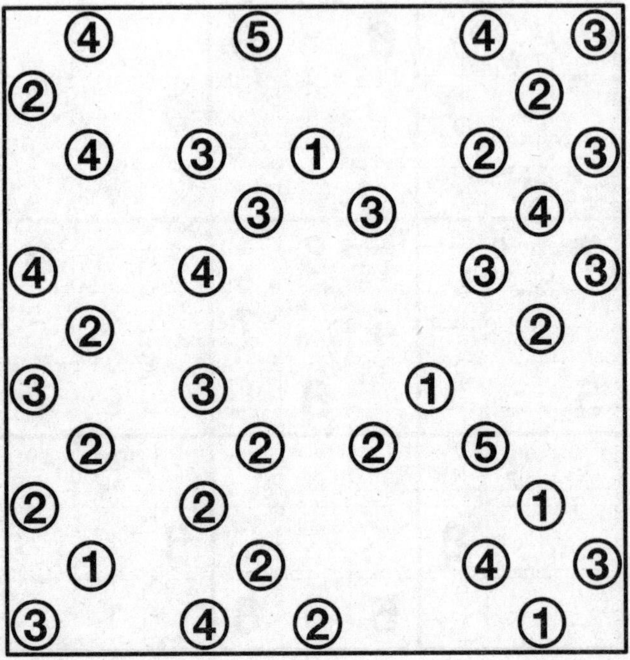

Instructions

Draw horizontal and vertical lines to represent bridges joining pairs of islands. Islands are indicated by circled numbers, where the number specifies the number of bridges that connect to that island.

- Any pair of islands may be joined by up to two bridges.
- Bridges may not cross either another bridge or an island.
- All islands must be joined together by the bridges, so you can travel to any island just by following the bridges.

 Your solving time: ____________

▪ Kropki ▪

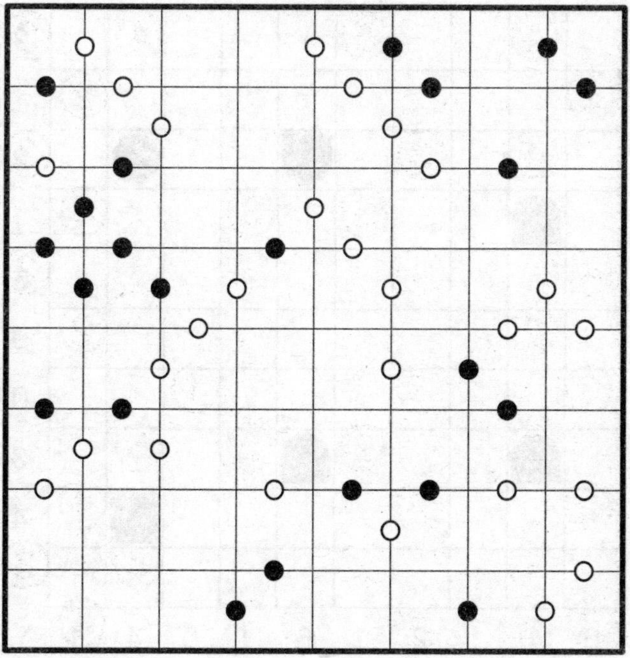

Instructions

Place digits from 1 to 8 once each in every row and column.

- Squares separated by a white dot must contain two consecutive numbers, such as 2 and 3, or 5 and 6.
- Squares separated by a black dot must contain numbers where one is twice the value of the other, such as 2 and 4.
- All possible dots are given – except where both a black and a white dot could be given, in which case only one dot is shown. The absence of a dot is therefore significant.

Your solving time: _____________

▪ Battleships ▪

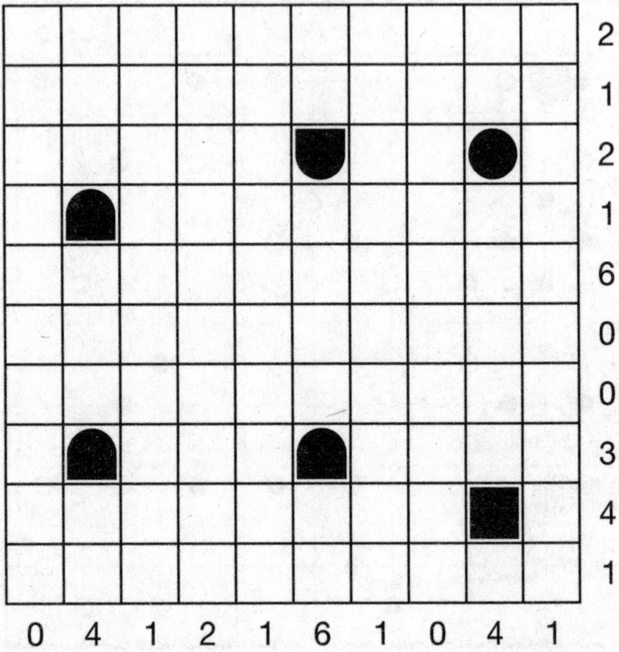

Instructions

Place the given set of 10 ships into the grid.

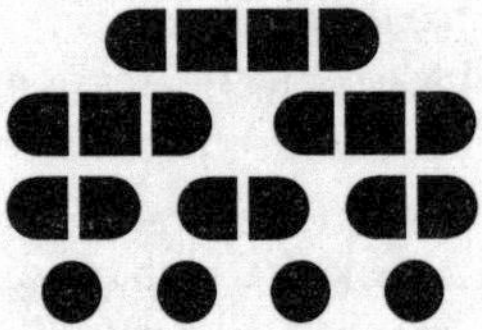

- Clues outside the grid reveal the number of squares in the corresponding row or column that contain a ship part.
- Ships cannot touch each other – not even diagonally.
- Some ship parts are already placed.
- Ships cannot be placed diagonally.

Your solving time: ____________

▪ Snake ▪

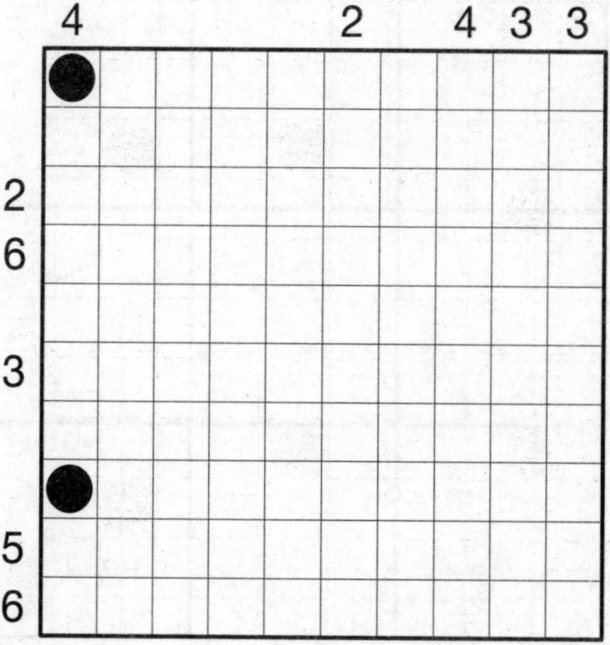

Instructions

Shade some squares to form a single snake that starts and ends at the squares marked with circles.

- A snake is a path of adjacent squares that does not branch or cross over itself.
- The snake does not touch itself – not even diagonally, except when turning a corner.
- Numbers outside the grid reveal the number of squares in their row or column that contain part of the snake.

Your solving time: ______________

▪ Quad Pencil-mark Sudoku ▪

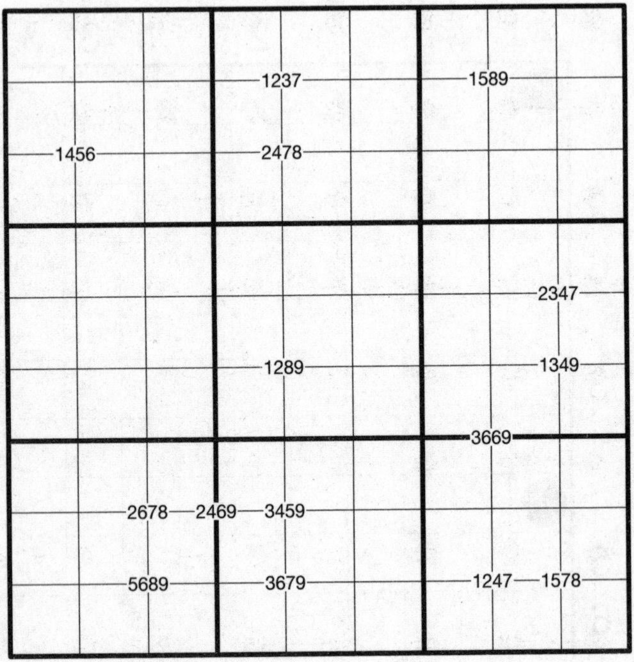

Instructions

Place a digit from 1 to 9 into every square, so that each digit appears once in every row, column and bold-lined 3×3 box.

- Wherever four digits appear on the intersection of four squares, those digits must be placed into those four squares in some order.

Your solving time: ____________

▪ Fences ▪

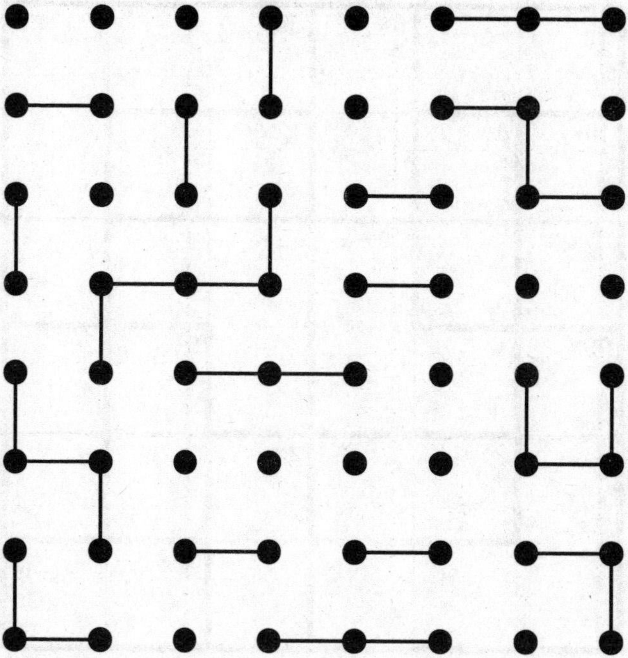

Instructions

Join all of the dots so as to form a single loop.

- The loop does not cross over or touch itself at any point.
- The loop can only consist of horizontal and diagonal lines between dots.

Your solving time: ____________

▪ Calcudoku ▪

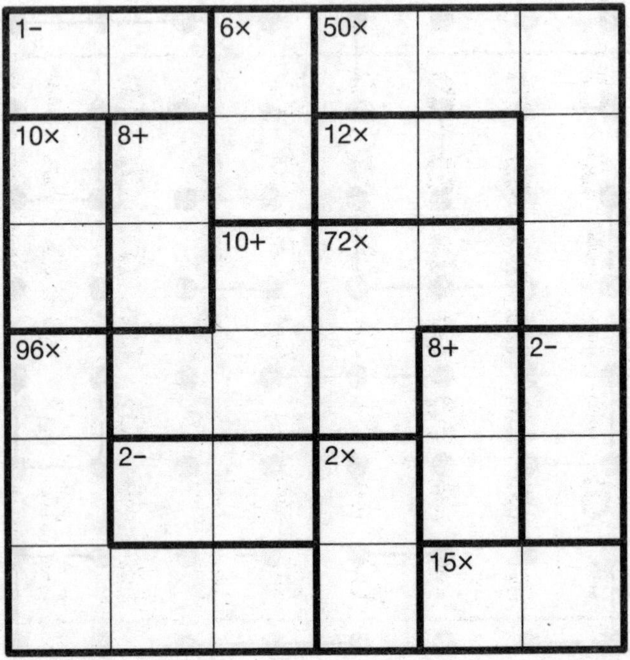

Instructions

Place a digit from 1 to 6 into every square, so that no digit repeats in any row or column.

- The value at the top-left of each bold-lined region must result when all of the numbers in that region have the given operation (+, –, ×, ÷) applied between them. For – and ÷ operations begin with the largest number in the region and then subtract or divide by the other numbers in any order.

Your solving time: ____________

▪ Dominoes ▪

0	5	6	2	2	0	5	1
3	0	0	2	3	2	6	4
1	2	4	5	0	6	6	4
1	5	3	4	0	2	6	5
1	5	2	4	5	5	6	3
6	6	1	4	4	0	1	3
1	4	1	3	3	0	2	3

Instructions

Draw solid lines to divide the grid up to form a complete set of standard dominoes, with exactly one of each domino.

- A '0' represents a blank on a traditional domino.
- Use the check-off chart to help you keep track of which dominoes you've placed.

0	1	2	3	4	5	6	
							0
							1
							2
							3
							4
							5
							6

Your solving time: ____________

▪ King's Journey ▪

				13			
18	16		14		30		
	21				10		
				52		32	
48	26						2
		50			63	54	1
	46	42		64		58	
45			40				57

Instructions

Write a number in each of the empty squares so that the grid contains every number from 1 to 64 exactly once.

- Place the numbers so that there is a route from 1 to 64 that visits every grid square exactly once in increasing numerical order, moving only left, right, up, down or diagonally between touching squares.

 Your solving time: __________

▪ Skyscrapers ▪

		4		3		
						3
3						
						4
	1					

Instructions

Place a digit from 1 to 5 into every square, so that no digit repeats in any row or column inside the grid.

- Each clue number outside the grid gives the number of digits that are 'visible' from that point, looking along that clue's row or column. A digit is visible unless there is a higher digit preceding it, reading from the clue along the row or column. E.g. the clue to the left of 14235 would be 3, since 1, 4 and 5 are visible, but 2 and 3 are obscured by 4.

Your solving time: ____________

▪ Four in a Row ▪

O		X		X		X	
X				O		O	O
X		X					O
	X	X	O			O	
X				O	X		
X		X	X		X		X
		O			X		
		X	X			O	O

Instructions

Place either an × or an o into every empty square.

- Complete the grid *without* forming any lines of four or more ×s or os.
- Lines can be formed in horizontal, vertical and diagonal directions.

 Your solving time: ____________

▪ Slitherlink ▪

3	2	3	2	3		0	
2	3		3		1		0
1		0		1		3	2
2	3		3		1	1	3
2	1	1		3		3	1
2	1		2		1		1
3		3		3		2	1
	0		2	3	2	3	1

Instructions

Draw a single loop by connecting together some, but not necessarily all, dots so that each numbered square has the specified number of adjacent line segments.

- Dots can only be joined by horizontal or vertical lines.
- The loop cannot touch, cross or overlap itself in any way.

Your solving time: ______________

▪ Walls ▪

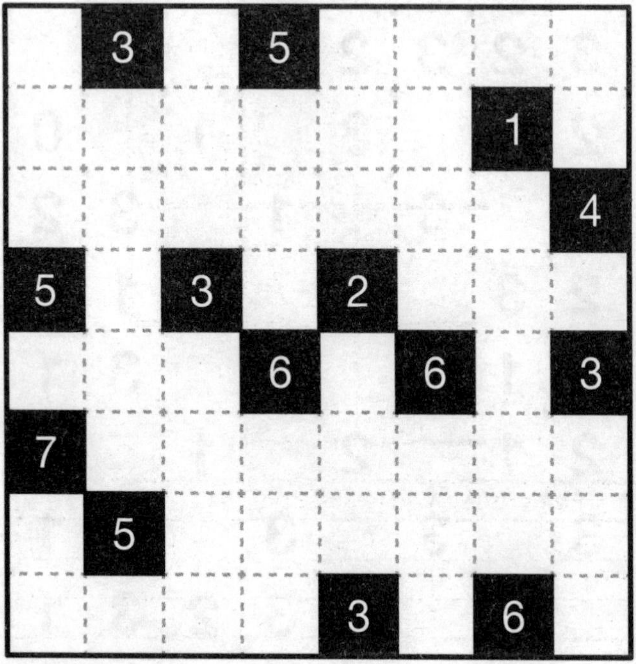

Instructions

Draw a horizontal or vertical line across the full width or height of the centre of every white square.

- The total length of all lines touching each black square must be equal to the number printed on that cell.
- The length of a line is defined as the number of squares it covers.
- Some lines may be shared between black squares; other lines may not touch any black squares.

Your solving time: ____________

▪ Written Logic ▪

		Destination			Time		
		Sandville	Seatown	Shellbury	15:10	15:40	16:00
Platform	1						
	2						
	3						
Time	15:10						
	15:40						
	16:00						

Platform	Destination	Time

Train Timetable

Three trains at a station are on platforms 1, 2 and 3, with one going to Shellbury, another to Seatown and one to Sandville. They leave at 15:10, 15:40 and 16:00. Given the following, what is the platform, time and destination of each train?

- The train for Seatown is leaving after the platform 3 train.
- The train leaving at 15:10 is on a lower platform number than the train for Shellbury.
- The train on platform 2 is not going to Seatown.

Your solving time: ____________

▪ Path Finder ▪

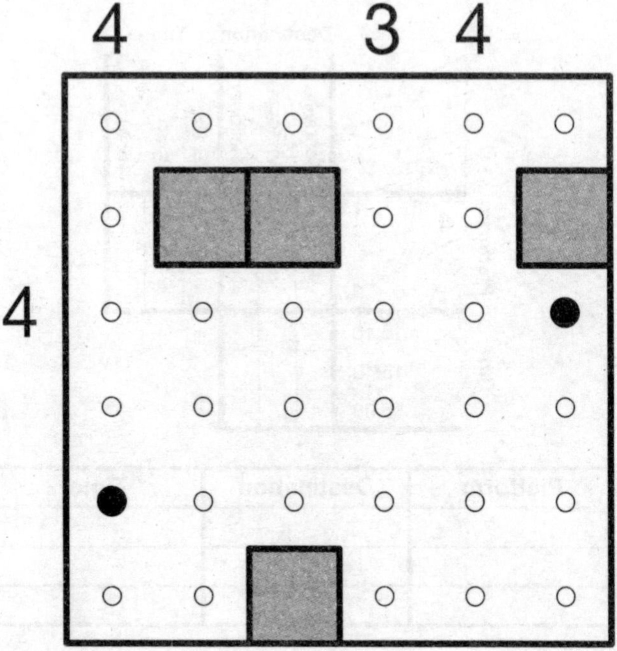

Instructions

Join some of the dots to form a single path which does not touch or cross itself at any point.

- The start and end of the path are indicated by black dots.
- Numbers outside the grid specify the number of dots in their row or column that are visited by the path.
- The path can't touch or cross over any of the shaded boxes.
- The path is constructed only of horizontal and vertical line segments.

 Your solving time: ____________

▪ Sudoku 3D Star ▪

Instructions

Place a digit from 1 to 8 into each empty square, so that no digit repeats in any row or column of 8 squares, or any bold-lined 4×2 or 2×4 box.

- Rows and columns start at one edge of the grid and follow along the same row or column until they reach half way across the grid; then they bend with the 3D surface and continue until they reach a different edge of the grid.

Your solving time: ____________

▪ Loop Finder ▪

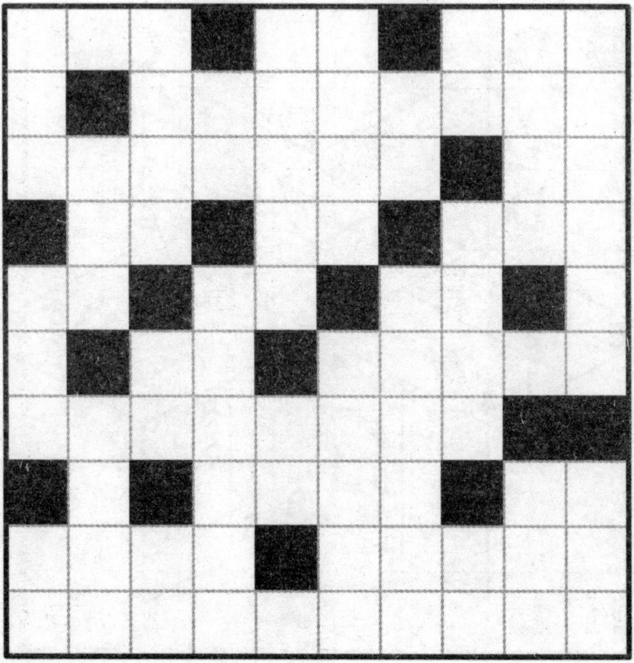

Instructions

Draw a single loop which visits every white square exactly once.

- The loop cannot touch or cross over either itself or a black square at any point.
- The loop consists only of horizontal and vertical line segments.

Your solving time: ____________

▪ Touchy ▪

D	G					C	A
			G	D			
	D					H	
		E			B		
		A			H		
	H					B	
			E	B			
H	E					D	B

Instructions

Place a letter from A to H into every square, so that no letter repeats in any row or column.

- Identical letters cannot be in diagonally touching squares.

▪ Frame Sudoku ▪

	9	3	9	5	10	6	
13							8
8							13
6							15
15							6
7							14
14							7
	6	10	5	9	4	8	

Instructions

Place a digit from 1 to 6 into every square, so that no digit repeats in any row or column.

- Clue numbers outside the grid give the sum of all the digits that are in the adjacent 3×2 box *and* that are in the same row or column as the clue.

Your solving time: ____________

▪ Binary Placement ▪

0	0		0				
1			0			0	
		0		1			
	0		1		1	1	
	1	0		1		0	
			0		1		
	1			0			0
				0		0	0

Instructions

Place 0 or 1 in every empty square so that there are an equal number of each digit in every row and column.

- Reading along any row or column, there must not be more than two of the same digit in direct succession. For example, 10011001 would be a valid row, while 10001101 would not be valid due to the three 0s in direct succession.

Your solving time: ____________

▪ Hanjie ▪

	5	7	8	8	8	8	8	8	7	5
2, 2										
4, 4										
10										
10										
10										
10										
8										
6										
4										
2										

Clue: Loving symbol

Instructions

Shade some squares while obeying the clues at the start of each row or column.

- The clues provide, in reading order, the length of every run of consecutive shaded squares in each row and column.
- There must be a gap of at least one empty square between each run of shaded squares in the same row or column.
- The finished puzzle will reveal a simple picture which fits the clue given beneath.

Your solving time: ______________

▪ Number Link ▪

1						2			
3			4					5	
		6				2			
				4					
								5	
	1	6			7				
	8	9		10	8		7		
							3		
							10		9

Instructions

Draw a set of separate paths, with one path connecting each pair of identical numbers.

- No more than one path can enter any square, and paths can only travel horizontally or vertically between squares.
- Paths cannot touch or cross one another.

Your solving time: ____________

▪ Kakuro ▪

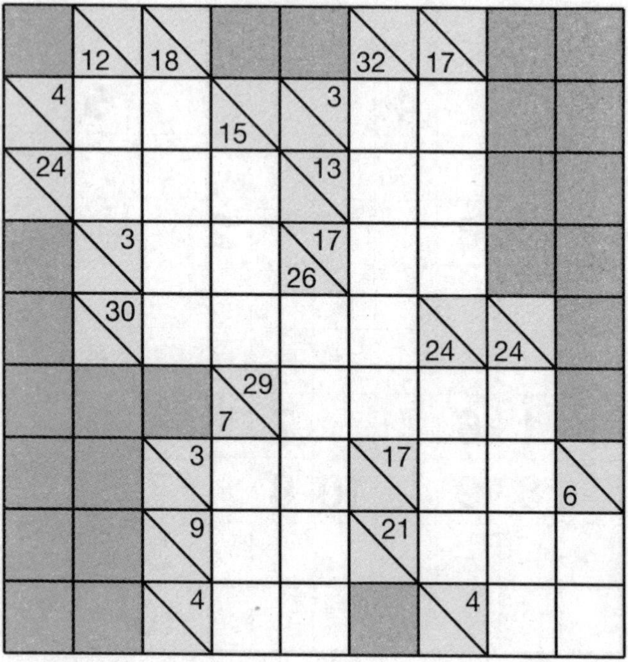

Instructions

Place a digit from 1 to 9 into each white square, and so that no placed digit repeats in any consecutive horizontal or vertical 'run' of squares.

- Each horizontal or vertical 'run' has a total given immediately to its left or above respectively. The digits in that run must add up to the given total.

Your solving time: ___________

▪ Arrow Sudoku ▪

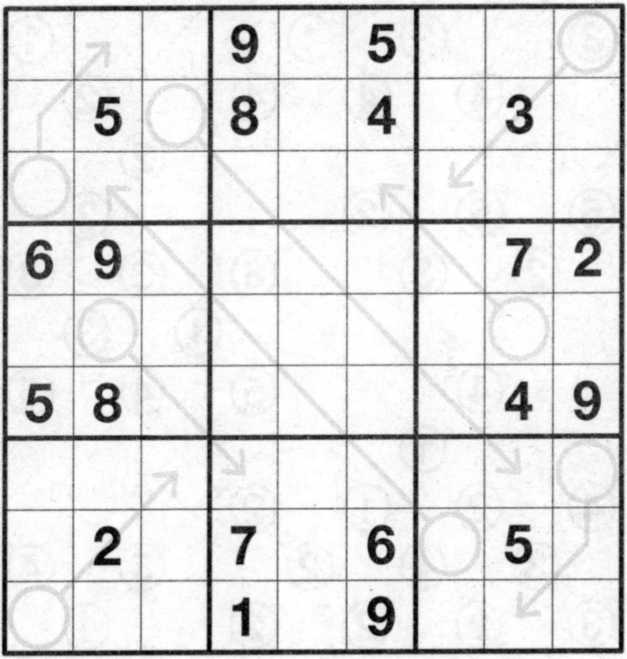

			9		5			
	5		8		4		3	
6	9						7	2
5	8						4	9
	2		7		6		5	
			1		9			

Instructions

Place a digit from 1 to 9 into every empty square, so that each digit appears once in every row, column and bold-lined 3×3 box.

- Circled squares must contain a value equal to the sum of the digits along their attached arrows.

Your solving time: ____________

▪ Bridges ▪

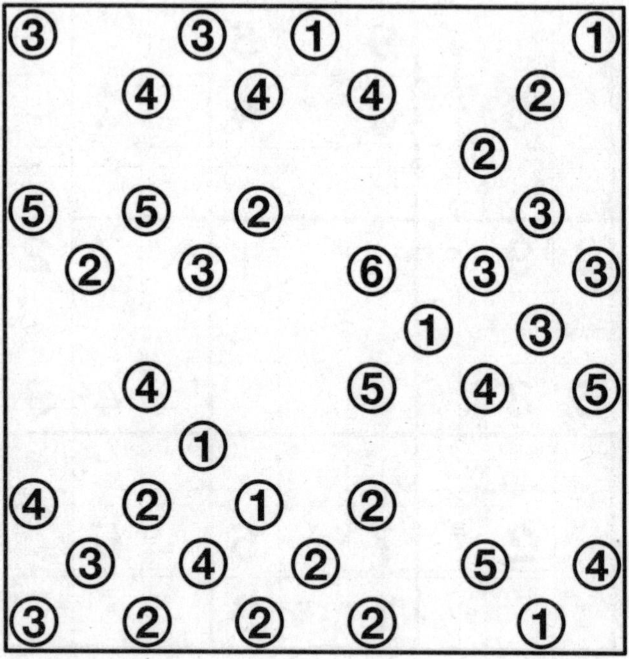

Instructions

Draw horizontal and vertical lines to represent bridges joining pairs of islands. Islands are indicated by circled numbers, where the number specifies the number of bridges that connect to that island.

- Any pair of islands may be joined by up to two bridges.
- Bridges may not cross either another bridge or an island.
- All islands must be joined together by the bridges, so you can travel to any island just by following the bridges.

Your solving time: ____________

▪ Kropki ▪

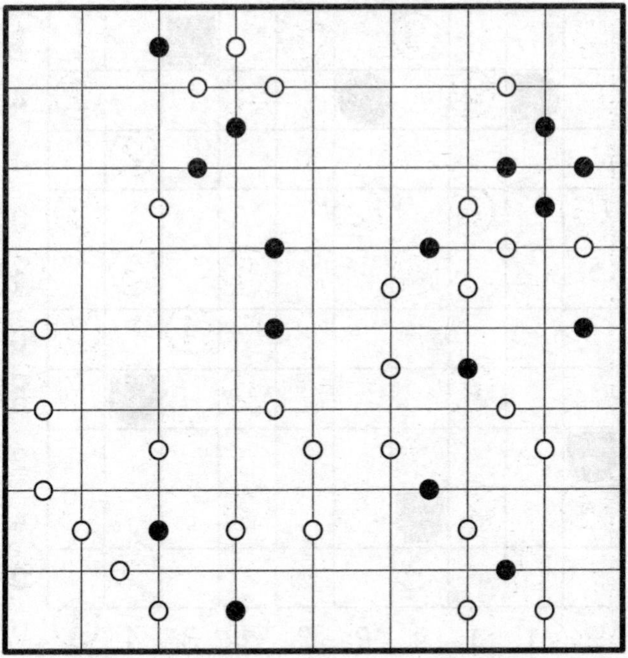

Instructions

Place digits from 1 to 8 once each in every row and column.

- Squares separated by a white dot must contain two consecutive numbers, such as 2 and 3, or 5 and 6.
- Squares separated by a black dot must contain numbers where one is twice the value of the other, such as 2 and 4.
- All possible dots are given – except where both a black and a white dot could be given, in which case only one dot is shown. The absence of a dot is therefore significant.

Your solving time: ______________

▪ Battleships ▪

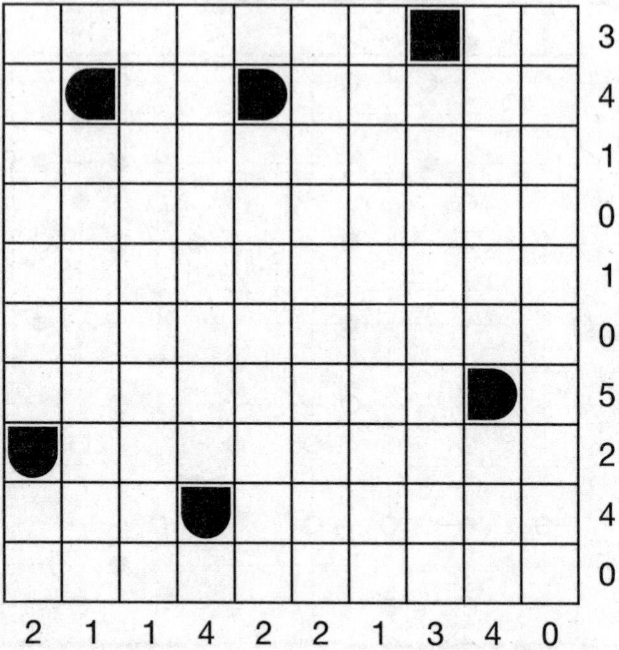

Instructions

Place the given set of 10 ships into the grid.

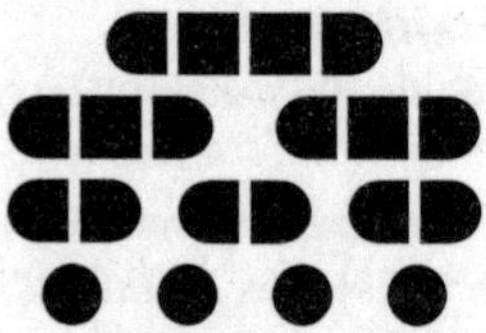

- Clues outside the grid reveal the number of squares in the corresponding row or column that contain a ship part.
- Ships cannot touch each other – not even diagonally.
- Some ship parts are already placed.
- Ships cannot be placed diagonally.

 Your solving time: ____________

▪ Snake ▪

	5	2	4	2			3		5	
									●	
3										
2										
4										
4										
8										
										●

Instructions

Shade some squares to form a single snake that starts and ends at the squares marked with circles.

- A snake is a path of adjacent squares that does not branch or cross over itself.
- The snake does not touch itself – not even diagonally, except when turning a corner.
- Numbers outside the grid reveal the number of squares in their row or column that contain part of the snake.

Your solving time: ______________

▪ Quad Pencil-mark Sudoku ▪

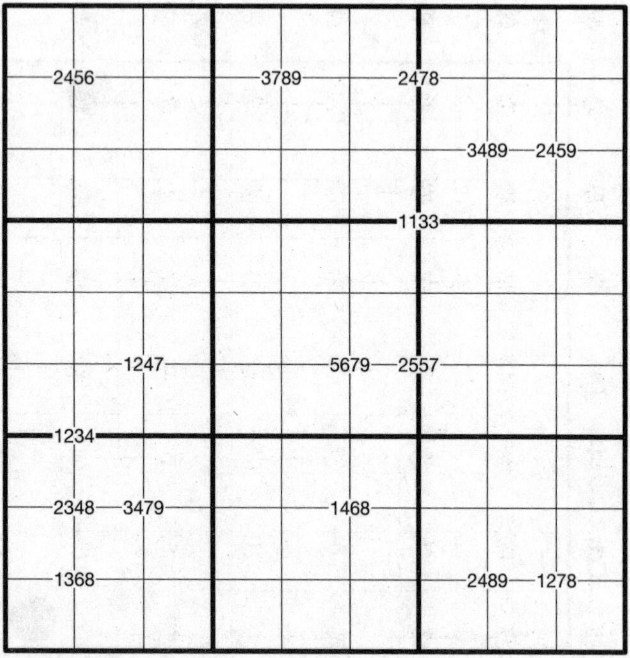

Instructions

Place a digit from 1 to 9 into every square, so that each digit appears once in every row, column and bold-lined 3×3 box.

- Wherever four digits appear on the intersection of four squares, those digits must be placed into those four squares in some order.

Your solving time: ____________

▪ Fences ▪

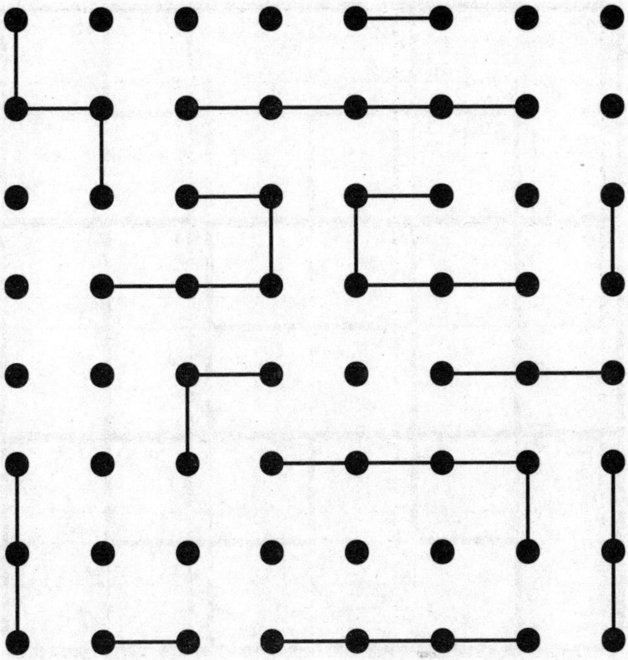

Instructions

Join all of the dots so as to form a single loop.

- The loop does not cross over or touch itself at any point.
- The loop can only consist of horizontal and diagonal lines between dots.

Your solving time: ______________

▪ Calcudoku ▪

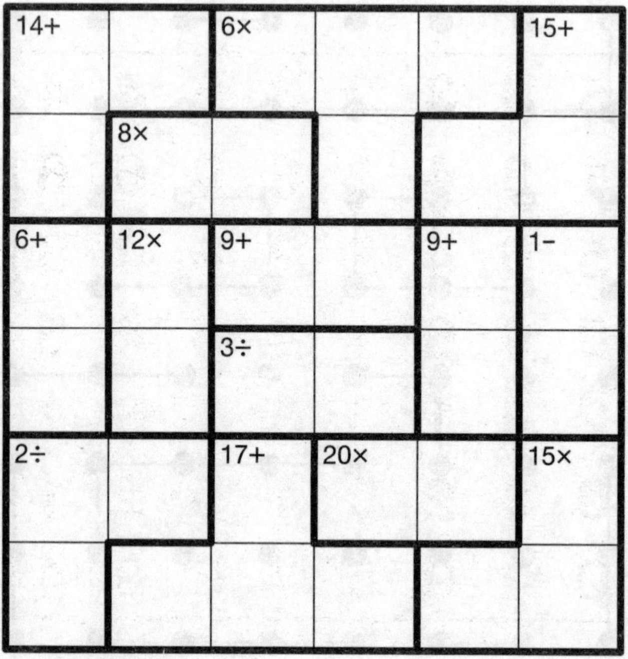

Instructions

Place a digit from 1 to 6 into every square, so that no digit repeats in any row or column.

- The value at the top-left of each bold-lined region must result when all of the numbers in that region have the given operation (+, –, ×, ÷) applied between them. For – and ÷ operations begin with the largest number in the region and then subtract or divide by the other numbers in any order.

 Your solving time: ____________

▪ Dominoes ▪

5	5	3	2	3	5	4	4
1	3	4	2	6	0	6	6
5	6	4	2	2	6	4	0
0	0	6	1	4	5	4	5
2	6	1	3	3	1	6	1
0	3	2	0	1	5	2	1
0	2	0	5	1	3	3	4

Instructions

Draw solid lines to divide the grid up to form a complete set of standard dominoes, with exactly one of each domino.

- A '0' represents a blank on a traditional domino.
- Use the check-off chart to help you keep track of which dominoes you've placed.

0	1	2	3	4	5	6	
							0
							1
							2
							3
							4
							5
							6

Your solving time: ______________

▪ King's Journey ▪

64						28	
1	63	61		11		27	
				5		26	
58		15			23		
56		16	21				34
	55		20			41	
	50			46			
52							38

Instructions

Write a number in each of the empty squares so that the grid contains every number from 1 to 64 exactly once.

- Place the numbers so that there is a route from 1 to 64 that visits every grid square exactly once in increasing numerical order, moving only left, right, up, down or diagonally between touching squares.

Your solving time: ____________

▪ Skyscrapers ▪

	2	3				
						2
1						
4						
						3
				4		

Instructions

Place a digit from 1 to 5 into every square, so that no digit repeats in any row or column inside the grid.

- Each clue number outside the grid gives the number of digits that are 'visible' from that point, looking along that clue's row or column. A digit is visible unless there is a higher digit preceding it, reading from the clue along the row or column. E.g. the clue to the left of 14235 would be 3, since 1, 4 and 5 are visible, but 2 and 3 are obscured by 4.

Your solving time: ______________

▪ Four in a Row ▪

	X	O			X		
X	X			X	O	O	X
					O		
X		X	O		X	O	
		X					O
X			O		O		
X	X	O	O				
	O		O			X	O

Instructions

Place either an × or an o into every empty square.

- Complete the grid *without* forming any lines of four or more ×s or os.
- Lines can be formed in horizontal, vertical and diagonal directions.

Your solving time: ____________

▪ Slitherlink ▪

3	3	3	2	3		2	3
2		1		2	3		2
1	2	2	3				3
	1			2	3	2	3
3	2	3	2			2	
2				2	2	2	3
3		3	1		2		2
3	2		2	2	3	3	1

Instructions

Draw a single loop by connecting together some, but not necessarily all, dots so that each numbered square has the specified number of adjacent line segments.

- Dots can only be joined by horizontal or vertical lines.
- The loop cannot touch, cross or overlap itself in any way.

Your solving time: ____________

▪ Walls ▪

			5				4
6					4		
			1				2
	7			4			
			5			7	
2				2			
		1					4
4				6			

Instructions

Draw a horizontal or vertical line across the full width or height of the centre of every white square.

- The total length of all lines touching each black square must be equal to the number printed on that cell.
- The length of a line is defined as the number of squares it covers.
- Some lines may be shared between black squares; other lines may not touch any black squares.

 Your solving time: ____________

▪ Written Logic ▪

		How many			Drink		
		2	3	5	Milk	Coffee	Orange juice
Meal	Breakfast						
	Lunch						
	Dinner						
Time	Milk						
	Coffee						
	Orange juice						

Meal	How many	Drink

Cookie Jar

You buy a packet of 10 chocolate-chip cookies, eating some with breakfast, some with lunch and the rest with dinner. At the meals you eat them with a glass of milk, a coffee or a glass of orange juice. How many cookies do you have at each meal, and what did you drink with them?

- You have the most cookies at lunch.
- You have milk with two cookies.
- You have orange juice the meal after having three cookies.

Your solving time: ____________

▪ Path Finder ▪

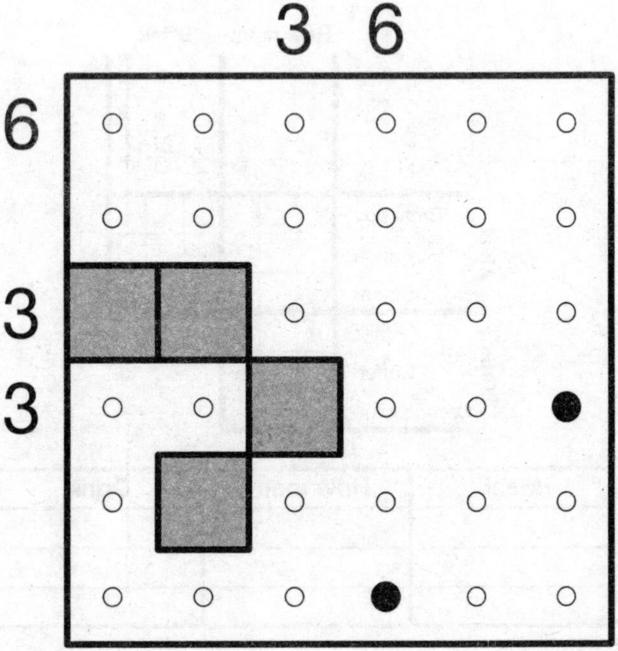

Instructions

Join some of the dots to form a single path which does not touch or cross itself at any point.

- The start and end of the path are indicated by black dots.
- Numbers outside the grid specify the number of dots in their row or column that are visited by the path.
- The path can't touch or cross over any of the shaded boxes.
- The path is constructed only of horizontal and vertical line segments.

Your solving time: ____________

▪ Sudoku 3D Star ▪

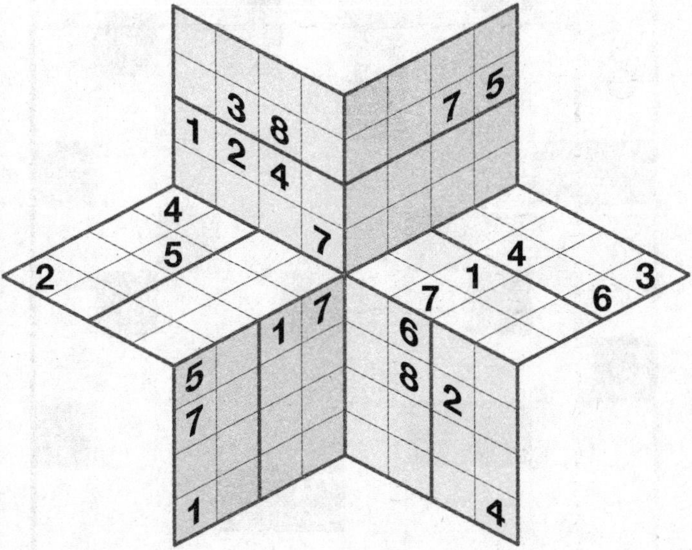

Instructions

Place a digit from 1 to 8 into each empty square, so that no digit repeats in any row or column of 8 squares, or any bold-lined 4×2 or 2×4 box.

- Rows and columns start at one edge of the grid and follow along the same row or column until they reach half way across the grid; then they bend with the 3D surface and continue until they reach a different edge of the grid.

Your solving time: ____________

▪ Loop Finder ▪

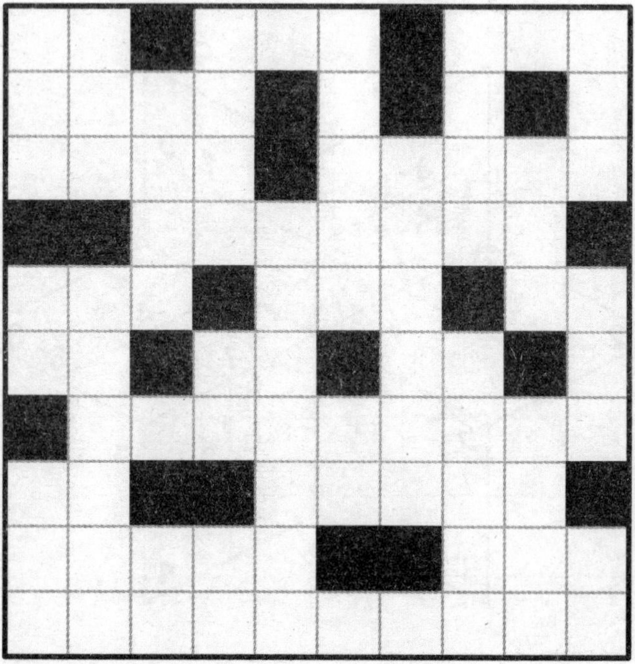

Instructions

Draw a single loop which visits every white square exactly once.

- The loop cannot touch or cross over either itself or a black square at any point.
- The loop consists only of horizontal and vertical line segments.

Your solving time: ___________

▪ Touchy ▪

B	E					G	H
			G	B			
	A	H			D	B	
	C	E			F	H	
			F	D			
F	B					D	A

Instructions
Place a letter from A to H into every square, so that no letter repeats in any row or column.

• Identical letters cannot be in diagonally touching squares.

▪ Frame Sudoku ▪

	8	6	7	4	11	6	
8							13
13							8
8							13
13							8
8							13
13							8
	8	4	9	8	5	8	

Instructions

Place a digit from 1 to 6 into every square, so that no digit repeats in any row or column.

- Clue numbers outside the grid give the sum of all the digits that are in the adjacent 3×2 box *and* that are in the same row or column as the clue.

Your solving time: ____________

▪ Binary Placement ▪

				1			1
	0				1		0
0	0		1		1		1
					0	1	0
1	0	1					
0		1		1		1	1
1		0				0	
1			1				

Instructions

Place 0 or 1 in every empty square so that there are an equal number of each digit in every row and column.

- Reading along any row or column, there must not be more than two of the same digit in direct succession. For example, 10011001 would be a valid row, while 10001101 would not be valid due to the three 0s in direct succession.

Your solving time: ______________

▪ Hanjie ▪

	2	4	4	4	5	5	5	4	4	4
1										
2										
3										
4										
1, 4										
3, 4										
7										
6										
4										
2										

Clue: Correct

Instructions

Shade some squares while obeying the clues at the start of each row or column.

- The clues provide, in reading order, the length of every run of consecutive shaded squares in each row and column.
- There must be a gap of at least one empty square between each run of shaded squares in the same row or column.
- The finished puzzle will reveal a simple picture which fits the clue given beneath.

 Your solving time: ______________

▪ Number Link ▪

								1	2
3	4				5				
6	3						7		8
							9		
		4			5				
					1				
			6	8	7	2	9		
	10							10	

Instructions

Draw a set of separate paths, with one path connecting each pair of identical numbers.

- No more than one path can enter any square, and paths can only travel horizontally or vertically between squares.
- Paths cannot touch or cross one another.

Your solving time: ____________

▪ Kakuro ▪

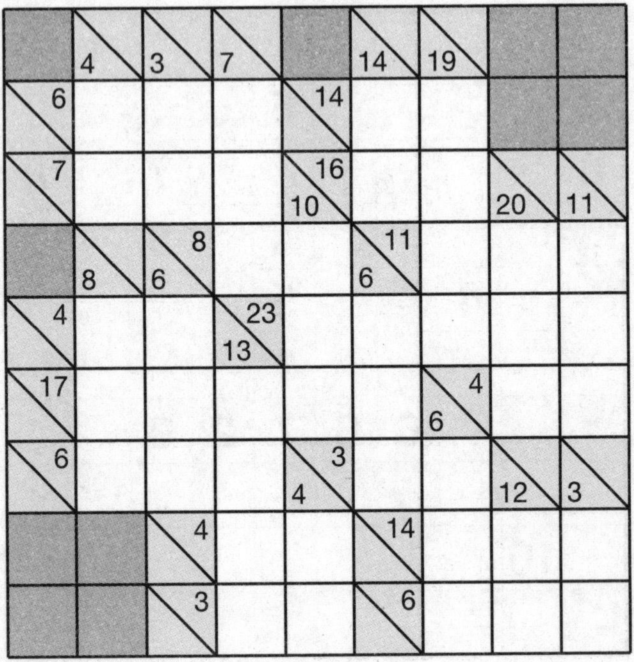

Instructions

Place a digit from 1 to 9 into each white square, and so that no placed digit repeats in any consecutive horizontal or vertical 'run' of squares.

- Each horizontal or vertical 'run' has a total given immediately to its left or above respectively. The digits in that run must add up to the given total.

Your solving time: ____________

▪ Arrow Sudoku ▪

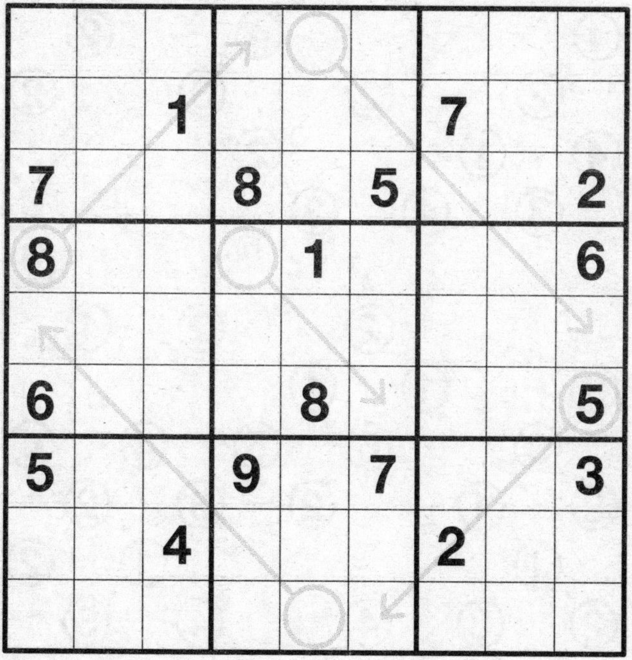

Instructions

Place a digit from 1 to 9 into every empty square, so that each digit appears once in every row, column and bold-lined 3×3 box.

- Circled squares must contain a value equal to the sum of the digits along their attached arrows.

Your solving time: ____________

▪ Bridges ▪

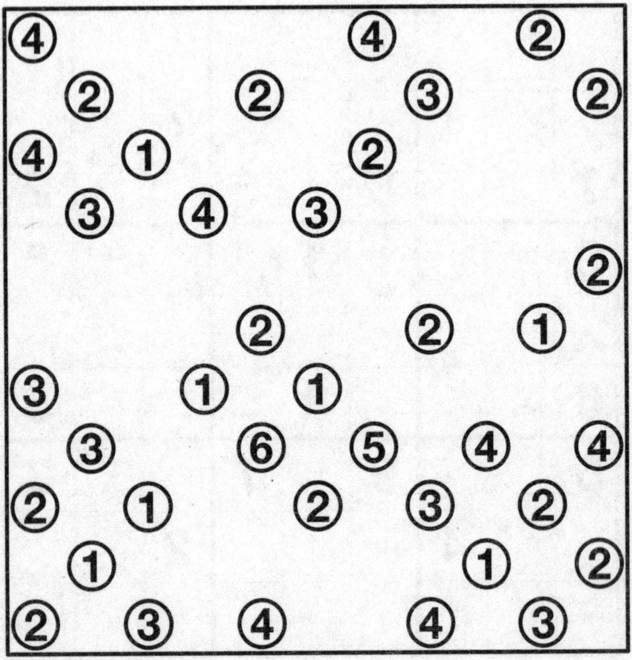

Instructions

Draw horizontal and vertical lines to represent bridges joining pairs of islands. Islands are indicated by circled numbers, where the number specifies the number of bridges that connect to that island.

- Any pair of islands may be joined by up to two bridges.
- Bridges may not cross either another bridge or an island.
- All islands must be joined together by the bridges, so you can travel to any island just by following the bridges.

 Your solving time: ___________

▪ Kropki ▪

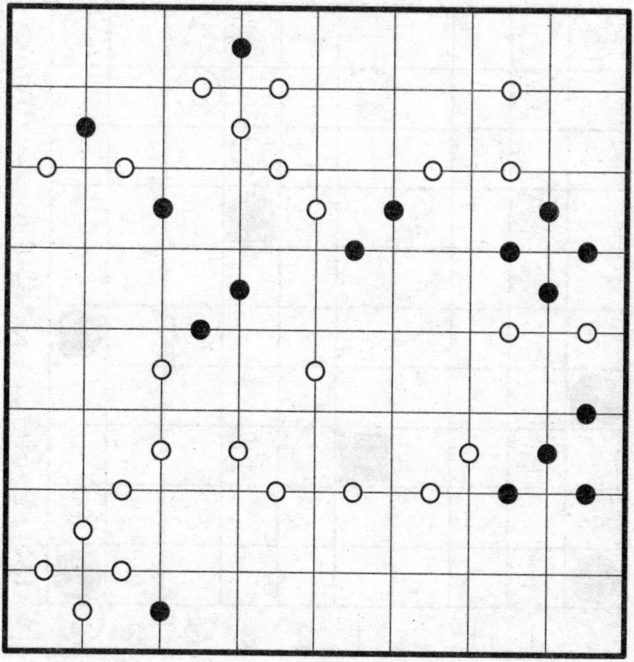

Instructions

Place digits from 1 to 8 once each in every row and column.

- Squares separated by a white dot must contain two consecutive numbers, such as 2 and 3, or 5 and 6.
- Squares separated by a black dot must contain numbers where one is twice the value of the other, such as 2 and 4.
- All possible dots are given – except where both a black and a white dot could be given, in which case only one dot is shown. The absence of a dot is therefore significant.

Your solving time: ___________

▪ Battleships ▪

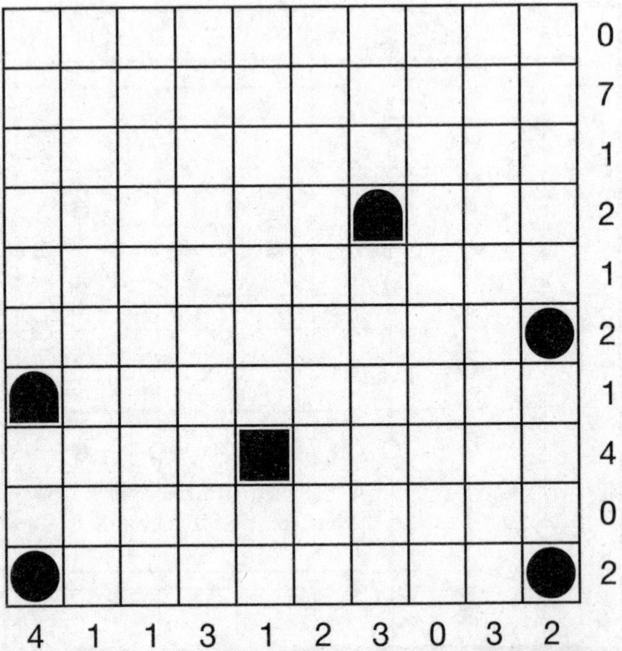

Instructions

Place the given set of 10 ships into the grid.

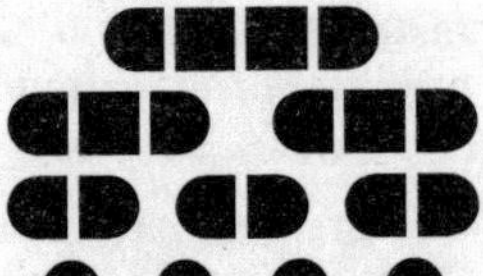

- Clues outside the grid reveal the number of squares in the corresponding row or column that contain a ship part.
- Ships cannot touch each other – not even diagonally.
- Some ship parts are already placed.
- Ships cannot be placed diagonally.

 Your solving time: ____________

▪ Snake ▪

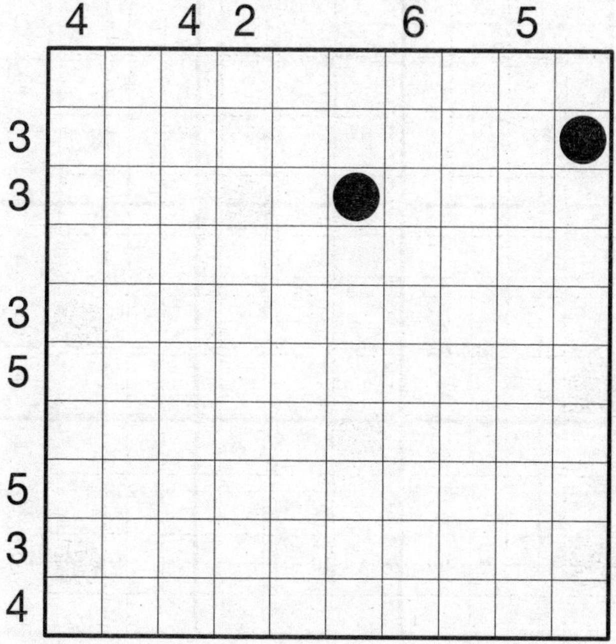

Instructions

Shade some squares to form a single snake that starts and ends at the squares marked with circles.

- A snake is a path of adjacent squares that does not branch or cross over itself.
- The snake does not touch itself – not even diagonally, except when turning a corner.
- Numbers outside the grid reveal the number of squares in their row or column that contain part of the snake.

Your solving time: ______________

▪ Quad Pencil-mark Sudoku ▪

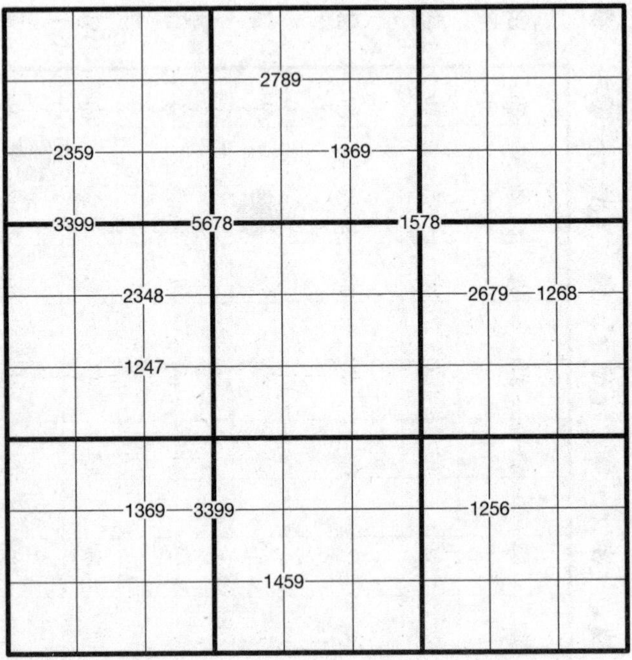

Instructions

Place a digit from 1 to 9 into every square, so that each digit appears once in every row, column and bold-lined 3×3 box.

- Wherever four digits appear on the intersection of four squares, those digits must be placed into those four squares in some order.

 Your solving time: ____________

▪ Fences ▪

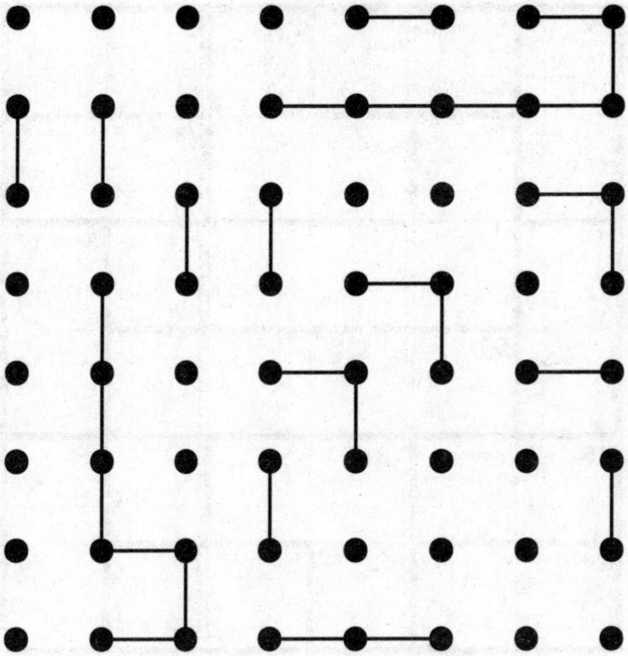

Instructions

Join all of the dots so as to form a single loop.

- The loop does not cross over or touch itself at any point.
- The loop can only consist of horizontal and diagonal lines between dots.

Your solving time: ____________

▪ Calcudoku ▪

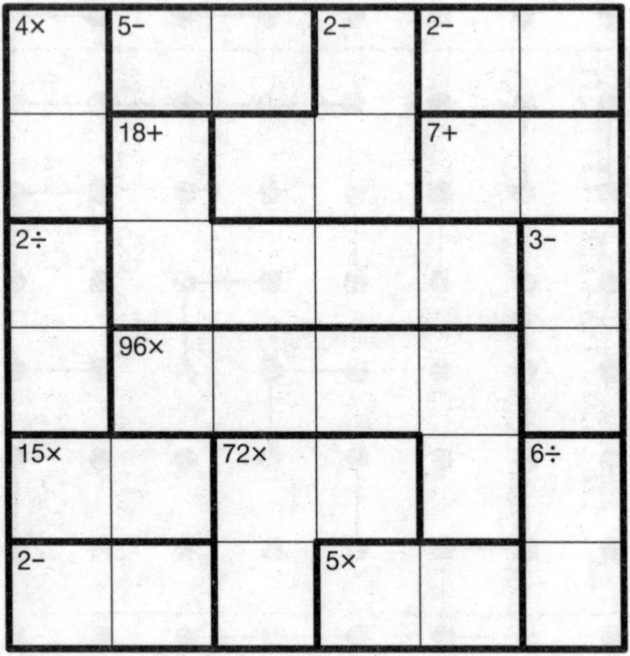

Instructions

Place a digit from 1 to 6 into every square, so that no digit repeats in any row or column.

- The value at the top-left of each bold-lined region must result when all of the numbers in that region have the given operation (+, −, ×, ÷) applied between them. For − and ÷ operations begin with the largest number in the region and then subtract or divide by the other numbers in any order.

 Your solving time: ____________

▪ Dominoes ▪

5	2	1	1	0	4	5	1
5	0	6	3	3	2	0	1
0	0	3	0	3	3	0	3
2	2	2	4	3	4	6	4
6	0	6	2	2	5	4	6
5	1	4	1	6	1	6	3
1	5	5	2	6	4	4	5

Instructions

Draw solid lines to divide the grid up to form a complete set of standard dominoes, with exactly one of each domino.

- A '0' represents a blank on a traditional domino.
- Use the check-off chart to help you keep track of which dominoes you've placed.

	0	1	2	3	4	5	6
0							
1							
2							
3							
4							
5							
6							

Your solving time: ____________

▪ King's Journey ▪

43				33	30	28	
		41					27
			35	10			
46	47	37	11				21
	49					15	18
	4				13		17
		2	55	57	58	61	62
	1					64	

Instructions

Write a number in each of the empty squares so that the grid contains every number from 1 to 64 exactly once.

- Place the numbers so that there is a route from 1 to 64 that visits every grid square exactly once in increasing numerical order, moving only left, right, up, down or diagonally between touching squares.

Your solving time: ______________

▪ Skyscrapers ▪

		1		2		
4						
3						
						5
				2		

Instructions

Place a digit from 1 to 5 into every square, so that no digit repeats in any row or column inside the grid.

- Each clue number outside the grid gives the number of digits that are 'visible' from that point, looking along that clue's row or column. A digit is visible unless there is a higher digit preceding it, reading from the clue along the row or column. E.g. the clue to the left of 14235 would be 3, since 1, 4 and 5 are visible, but 2 and 3 are obscured by 4.

Your solving time: ______________

▪ Four in a Row ▪

	O			O			O
O	O	O	X			O	O
O	O						O
O					X		
		O	X			O	X
X		O		O			X
		X		X		O	
X	X	O			O	O	O

Instructions

Place either an × or an o into every empty square.

- Complete the grid *without* forming any lines of four or more ×s or os.
- Lines can be formed in horizontal, vertical and diagonal directions.

 Your solving time: ____________

▪ Slitherlink ▪

3	2		2	2	3	2	3
2		2	1				3
3	2	3	2	1	3		3
3			3	2		1	
	3		3	1			2
3		0	2	2	2	2	1
3				3	1		3
3	1	1	2	2		0	1

Instructions

Draw a single loop by connecting together some, but not necessarily all, dots so that each numbered square has the specified number of adjacent line segments.

- Dots can only be joined by horizontal or vertical lines.
- The loop cannot touch, cross or overlap itself in any way.

Your solving time: ____________

■ Walls ■

Instructions

Draw a horizontal or vertical line across the full width or height of the centre of every white square.

- The total length of all lines touching each black square must be equal to the number printed on that cell.
- The length of a line is defined as the number of squares it covers.
- Some lines may be shared between black squares; other lines may not touch any black squares.

 Your solving time: ____________

▪ Written Logic ▪

		Temperature			Weather		
		10°	17°	20°	Clear skies	Rain	Hail
Day	Today						
	Tomorrow						
	Following day						
Weather	Clear skies						
	Rain						
	Hail						

Day	Temperature	Weather

Whatever the Weather

Some weather forecasts have been muddled up. You know it will be 10° on one day, 17° on another, and 20° on the remaining day. You also know rain is forecast one day, hail on another, and clear skies on the remaining day. What is the forecast for today, tomorrow and the day after?

- The 20° day is prior to the day with clear skies.
- Tomorrow will be warmer than the day with hail.
- It will not hail the day after tomorrow or on the 17° day.

Your solving time: ______________

▪ Solutions ▪

Page 7

9	5	6	8	4	3	2	1	7
1	8	3	2	9	7	5	4	6
2	4	7	5	1	6	3	9	8
4	1	5	7	8	2	9	6	3
6	7	2	9	3	5	1	8	4
3	9	8	1	6	4	7	2	5
5	6	4	3	2	9	8	7	1
8	3	9	6	7	1	4	5	2
7	2	1	4	5	8	6	3	9

Page 8

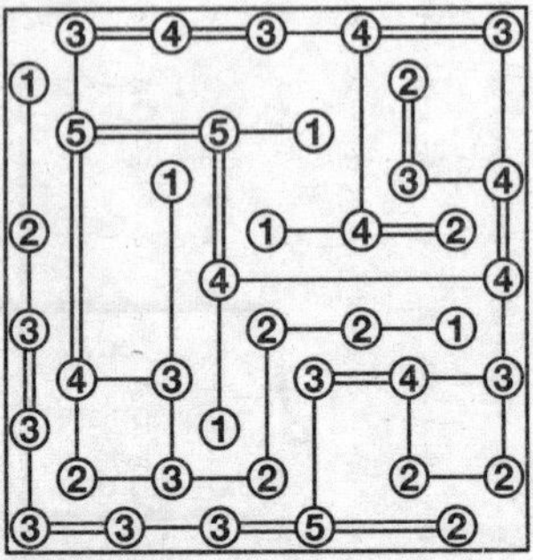

Page 9

5	3	7	2	6	4	1	8
8	6	2	4	5	3	7	1
3	2	1	7	8	6	5	4
1	4	5	6	2	7	8	3
4	8	6	1	7	2	3	5
2	1	3	8	4	5	6	7
7	5	4	3	1	8	2	6
6	7	8	5	3	1	4	2

Page 10

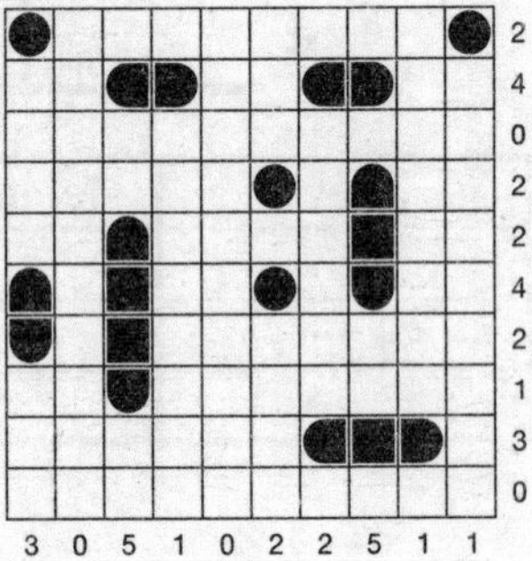

Page 11

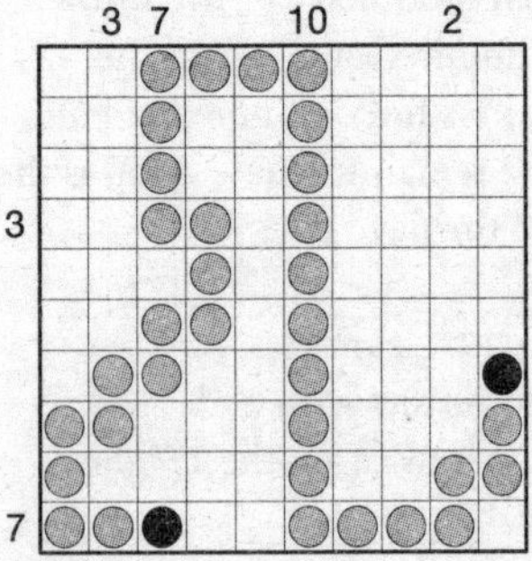

Page 12

9	1	5	6	8	3	2	4	7
6	7	8	9	2	4	5	1	3
2	4	3	5	1	7	6	9	8
7	9	4	1	6	2	8	3	5
3	5	1	4	7	8	9	6	2
8	2	6	3	5	9	4	7	1
1	3	9	2	4	5	7	8	6
5	6	7	8	9	1	3	2	4
4	8	2	7	3	6	1	5	9

▪ Solutions ▪

Page 13

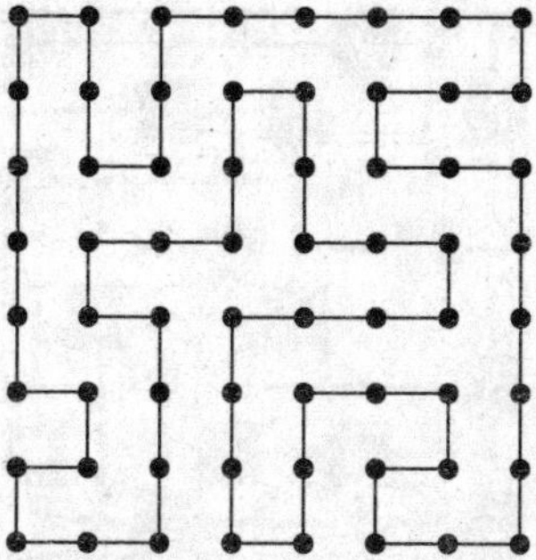

Page 14

11+ 3	2× 1	2	11+ 5	24× 4	6
2	7+ 3	4	6	9+ 1	5× 5
6	48× 4	7+ 5	2	3	1
20× 4	6	3÷ 1	3	5	24× 2
5	2	9+ 3	6× 1	6	4
5÷ 1	5	6	8× 4	2	3

Page 15

6	4	6	4	2	1	4	4
2	0	5	0	3	1	4	1
4	0	6	5	6	2	5	2
3	3	6	2	6	5	0	2
5	5	2	1	1	5	1	2
0	0	3	3	3	4	5	6
6	3	1	4	0	0	3	1

Page 16

35	36	37	54	55	60	61	62
34	52	53	38	56	57	59	63
31	33	51	49	39	58	1	64
32	30	29	50	48	40	42	2
21	20	27	28	47	41	43	3
19	22	26	25	46	44	4	5
17	18	23	24	45	11	6	8
16	15	14	13	12	10	9	7

Page 17

				3		
	3	4	5	1	2	
	2	5	4	3	1	4
2	4	3	1	2	5	1
4	1	2	3	5	4	
	5	1	2	4	3	
	1					

Page 18

X	X	O	O	O	X	O	X
O	O	X	X	O	X	X	X
X	O	O	O	X	X	O	O
O	O	O	X	O	O	X	X
O	X	O	X	X	O	X	X
O	X	X	O	O	O	X	O
X	O	X	O	X	X	O	O
O	X	X	X	O	X	X	O

▪ Solutions ▪

Page 19

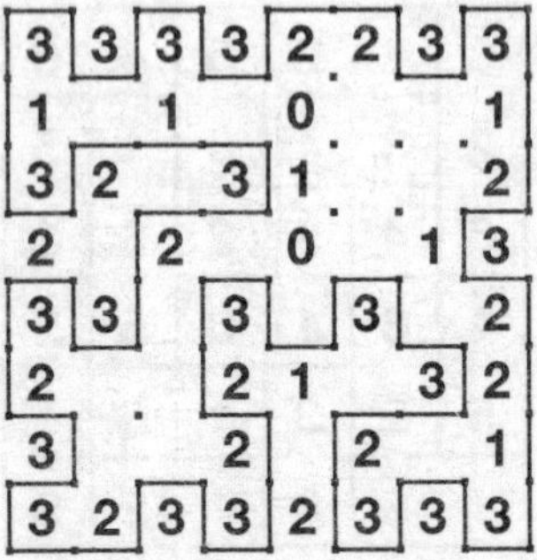

Page 20

Page 21

You ate toast and drank orange juice on Friday. You ate a bowl of cereal and drank coffee on Saturday. You ate fruit and drank milk on Sunday.

Page 22

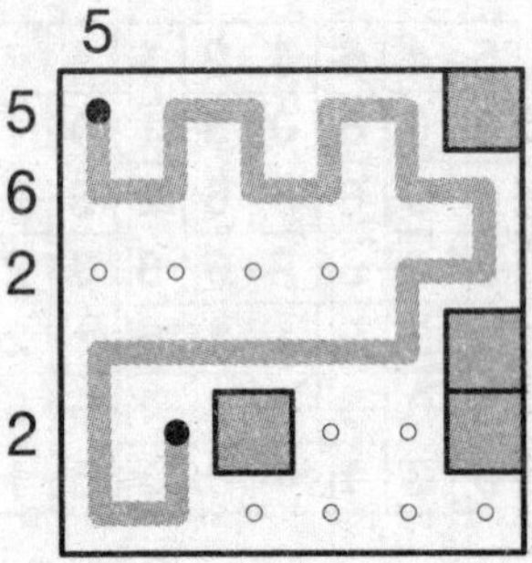

Page 23

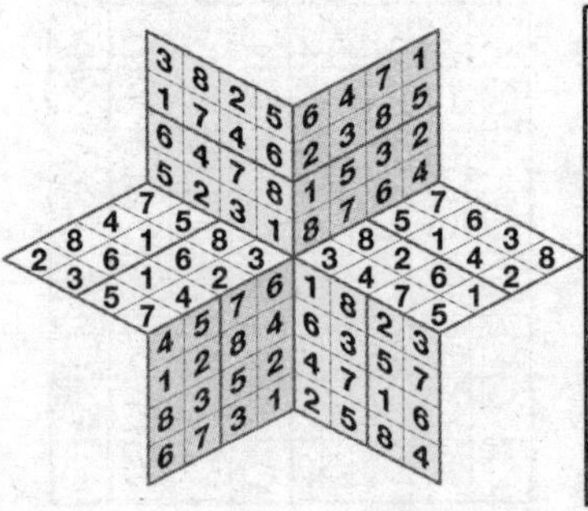

Page 24

▪ Solutions ▪

Page 25

A	D	H	F	B	E	G	C
F	C	B	G	A	D	H	E
B	E	D	H	C	G	F	A
H	F	C	A	D	B	E	G
G	A	E	B	F	H	C	D
C	H	G	D	E	A	B	F
E	B	A	C	G	F	D	H
D	G	F	E	H	C	A	B

Page 26

	7	5	9	6	6	9	
6	2	1	3	4	5	6	15
15	5	4	6	2	1	3	6
8	1	5	2	6	3	4	13
13	3	6	4	5	2	1	8
7	4	2	1	3	6	5	14
14	6	3	5	1	4	2	7
	10	5	6	4	10	7	

Page 27

0	0	1	0	1	0	1	1
0	1	0	1	0	0	1	1
1	0	1	0	1	1	0	0
0	1	0	0	1	0	1	1
1	0	1	1	0	1	0	0
0	0	1	0	1	1	0	1
1	1	0	1	0	0	1	0
1	1	0	1	0	1	0	0

Page 28

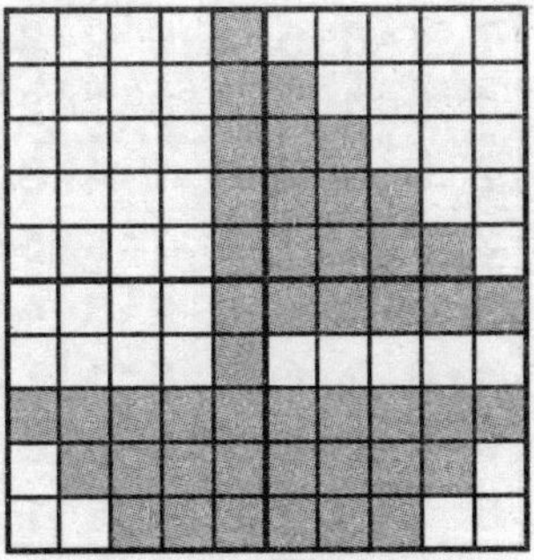

Page 29

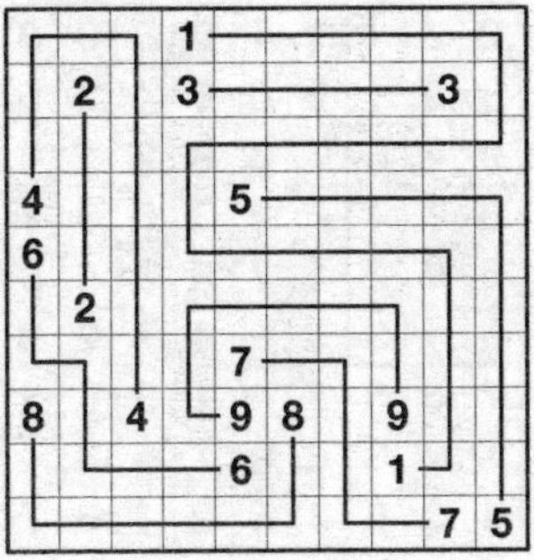

Page 30

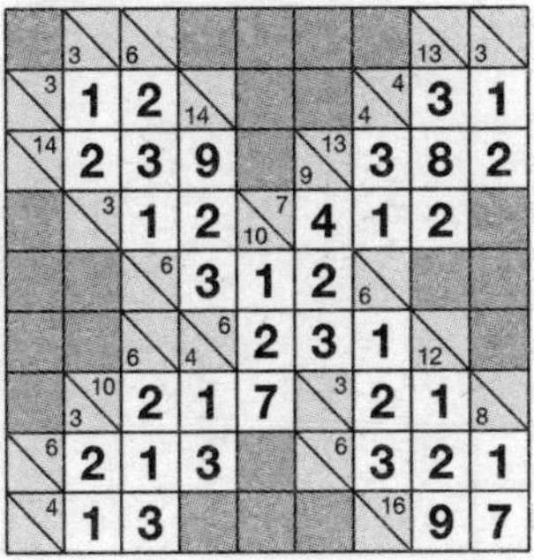

▪ Solutions ▪

Page 31

5	1	9	6	4	2	8	7	3
2	7	6	5	3	8	9	4	1
3	8	4	9	1	7	6	5	2
4	5	2	1	8	6	3	9	7
7	3	8	2	5	9	1	6	4
6	9	1	4	7	3	2	8	5
9	4	5	3	6	1	7	2	8
8	2	3	7	9	4	5	1	6
1	6	7	8	2	5	4	3	9

Page 32

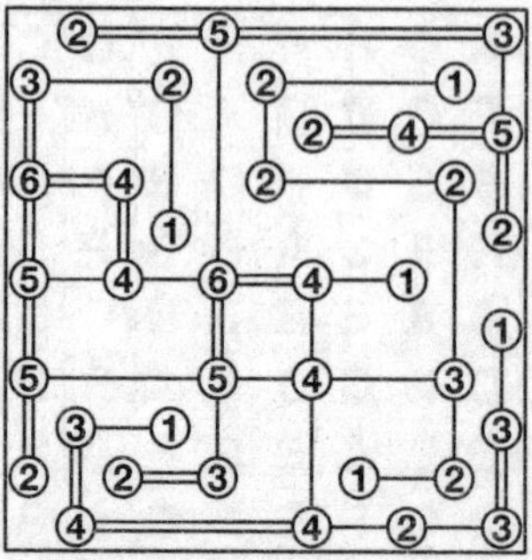

Page 33

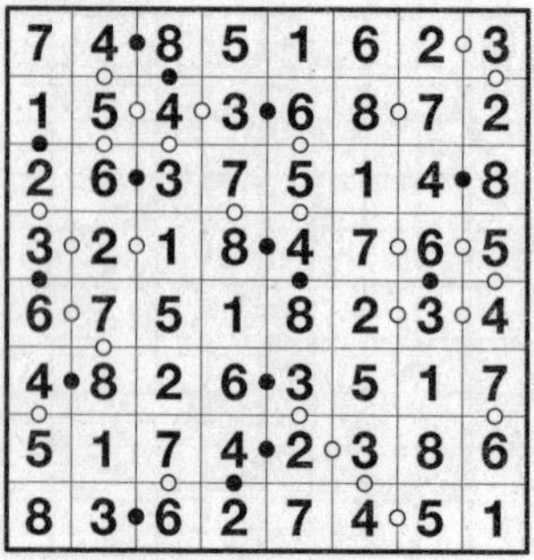

Page 34

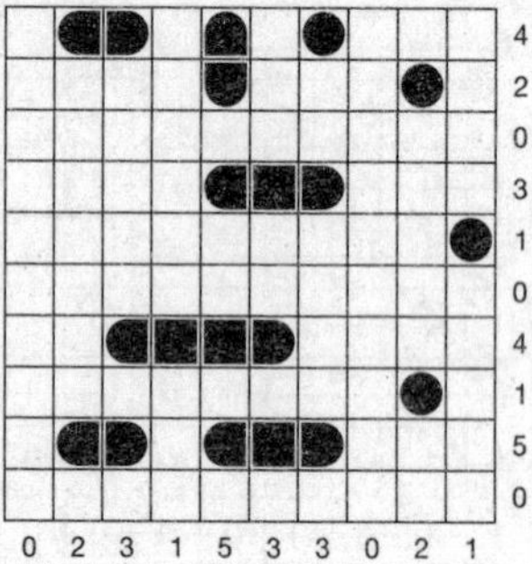

Page 35

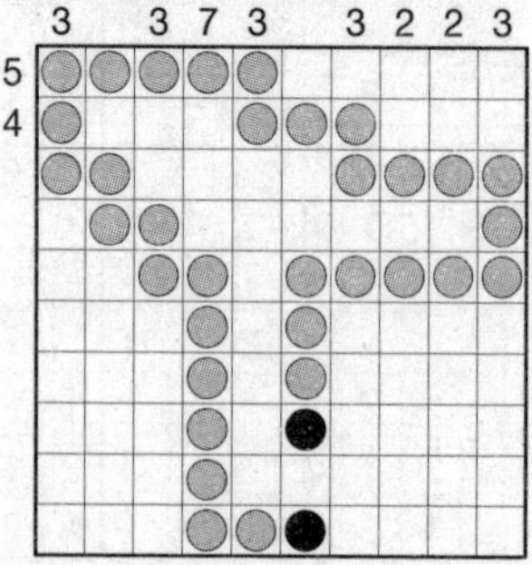

Page 36

2	6	7	4	1	5	8	9	3
3	8	1	2	6	9	4	7	5
9	4	5	7	3	8	2	1	6
8	7	4	9	2	3	6	5	1
5	9	2	1	7	6	3	4	8
6	1	3	5	8	4	7	2	9
7	5	6	3	4	1	9	8	2
1	2	8	6	9	7	5	3	4
4	3	9	8	5	2	1	6	7

▪ Solutions ▪

Page 37

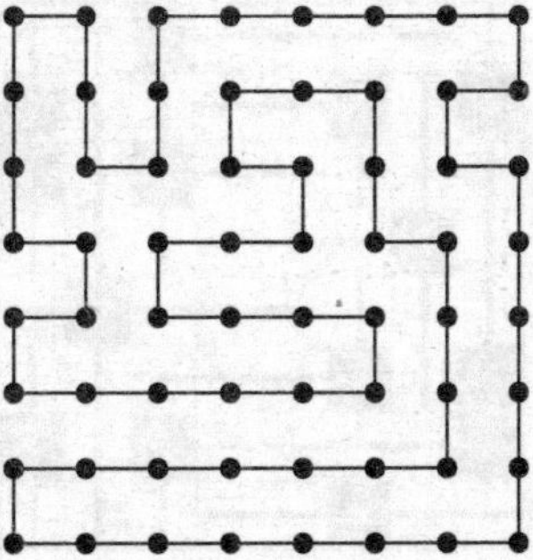

Page 38

2− 3	48× 6	4	2	6+ 5	1
5	2× 2	1	4+ 3	10+ 4	6
7+ 4	3− 3	6	1	11+ 2	5
2	1	10× 5	3− 6	3	4
24× 6	4	2	5÷ 5	1	5+ 3
4− 1	5	13+ 3	4	6	2

Page 39

6	0	5	1	2	1	5	1
4	2	3	5	0	1	4	2
3	4	5	4	2	3	0	2
5	0	0	6	6	6	1	4
5	4	2	2	1	6	0	4
1	4	1	3	3	5	5	2
3	3	6	0	6	3	6	0

Page 40

31	29	33	34	35	36	39	40
30	32	28	26	25	38	37	41
15	14	27	3	1	24	42	44
13	16	4	2	20	23	45	43
12	5	17	19	22	21	47	46
6	11	18	60	61	62	64	48
7	10	59	55	54	63	51	49
8	9	58	57	56	53	52	50

Page 41

	4		1	3		
2	2	1	5	3	4	
3	3	2	1	4	5	
3	1	4	3	5	2	
	4	5	2	1	3	2
	5	3	4	2	1	

Page 42

X	X	O	O	O	X	X	X
X	X	X	O	X	X	O	X
O	O	X	X	X	O	O	O
X	X	O	O	O	X	X	X
O	X	X	X	O	O	O	X
O	X	O	O	X	X	O	O
O	O	X	O	X	O	X	X
X	X	O	X	O	O	X	X

▪ Solutions ▪

Page 43

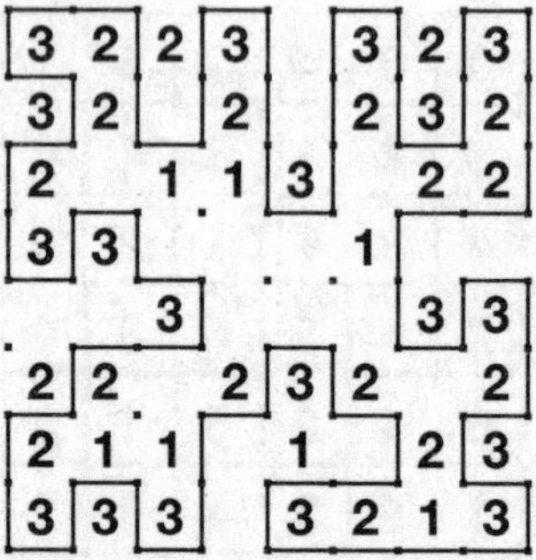

Page 44

Page 45

Patel is in first place and is cycling at 24mph. Thomson is in second place and is cycling at 28 mph. Walker is in third place and is cycling at 26 mph.

Page 46

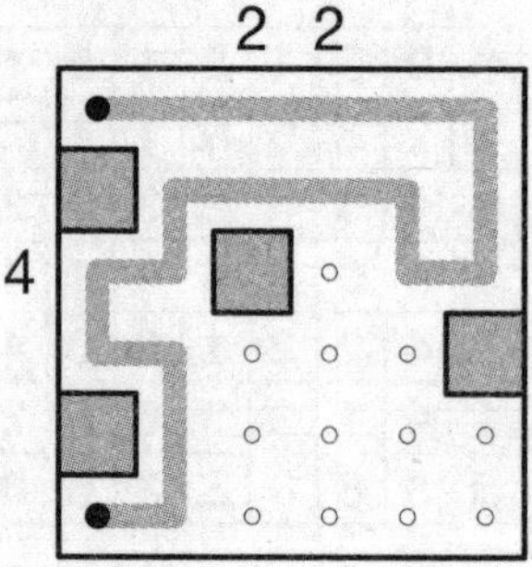

Page 47

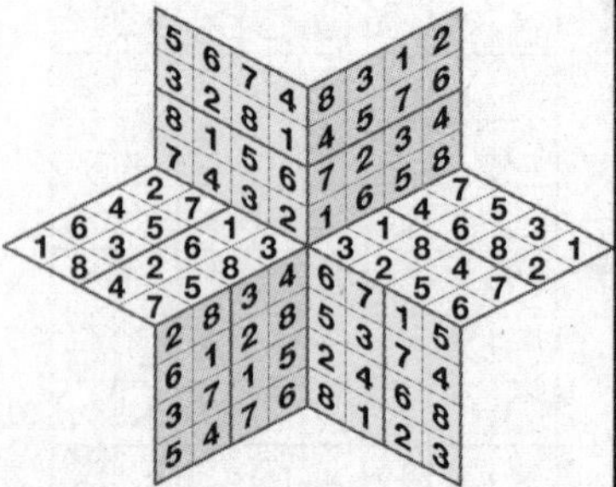

Page 48

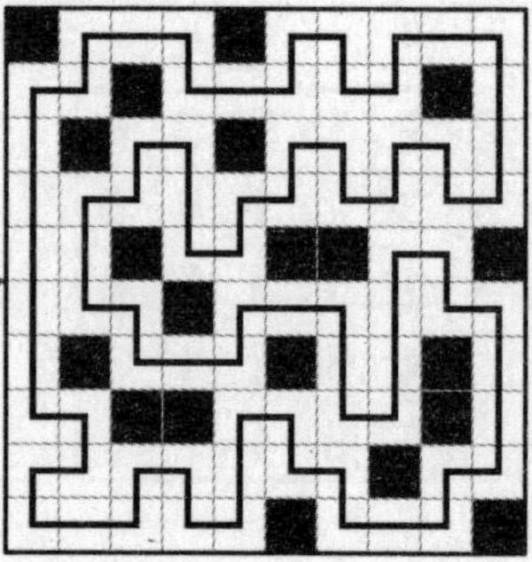

▪ Solutions ▪

Page 49

D	F	A	G	B	H	E	C
H	G	E	C	D	F	A	B
B	D	F	H	A	C	G	E
G	H	C	D	E	B	F	A
C	E	G	B	F	A	H	D
A	B	H	E	G	D	C	F
F	C	D	A	H	E	B	G
E	A	B	F	C	G	D	H

Page 50

	6	10	5	3	9	9	
13	5	6	2	1	4	3	8
8	1	4	3	2	5	6	13
8	3	1	4	5	6	2	13
13	6	2	5	3	1	4	8
8	4	3	1	6	2	5	13
13	2	5	6	4	3	1	8
	6	8	7	10	5	6	

Page 51

0	0	1	1	0	0	1	1
0	0	1	0	1	0	1	1
1	1	0	0	1	1	0	0
1	0	1	1	0	0	1	0
0	1	0	1	0	1	0	1
0	0	1	0	1	0	1	1
1	1	0	0	1	1	0	0
1	1	0	1	0	1	0	0

Page 52

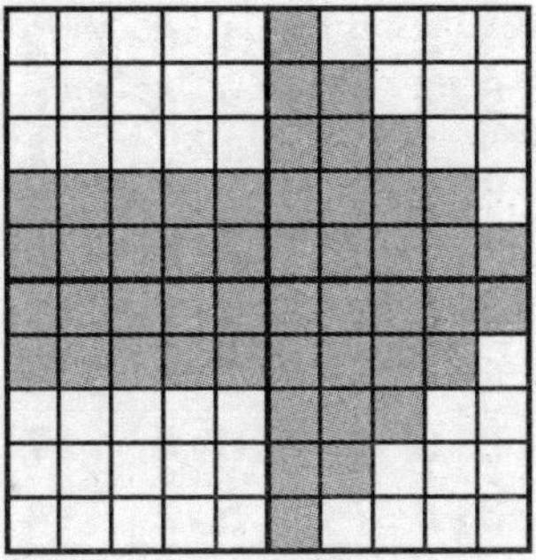

Page 53

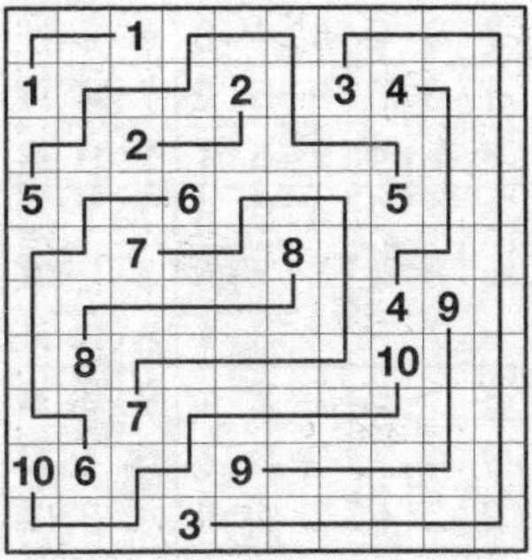

Page 54

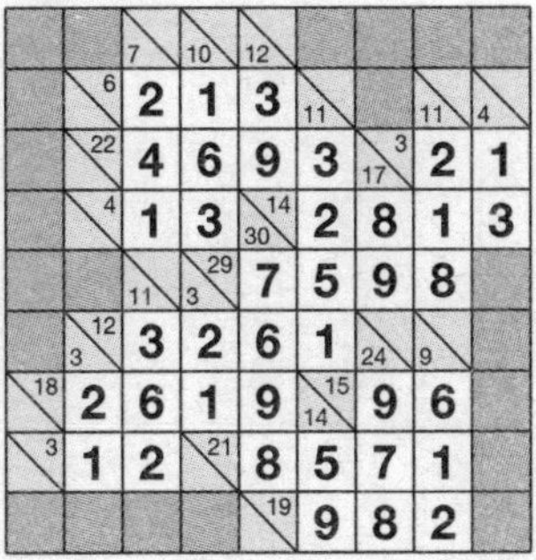

▪ Solutions ▪

Page 55

1	5	9	7	8	6	3	4	2
8	3	2	9	4	5	1	7	6
7	4	6	3	2	1	5	9	8
3	9	1	4	6	7	2	8	5
4	7	8	1	5	2	9	6	3
6	2	5	8	3	9	7	1	4
5	1	3	6	9	8	4	2	7
9	8	4	2	7	3	6	5	1
2	6	7	5	1	4	8	3	9

Page 56

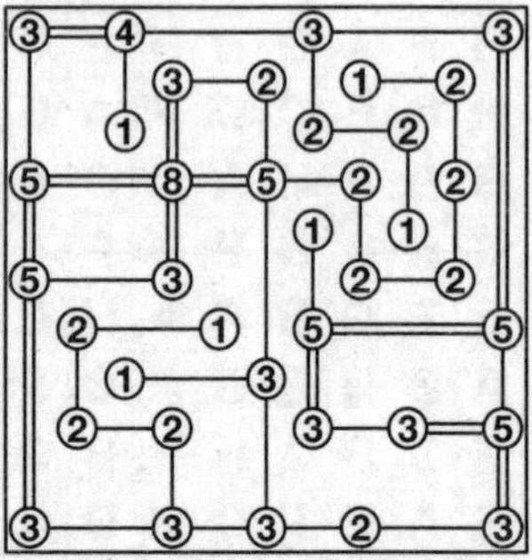

Page 57

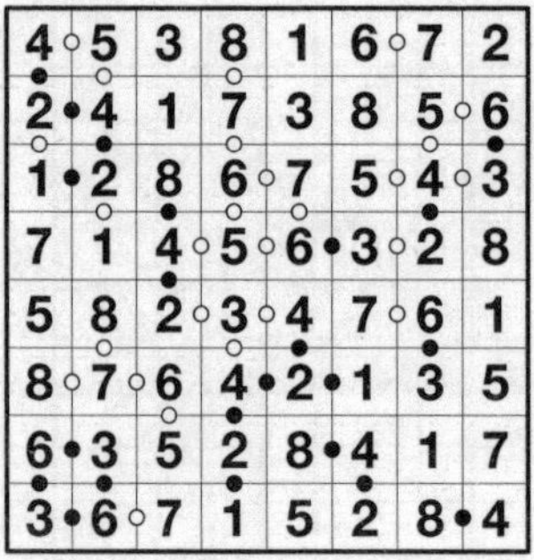

Page 58

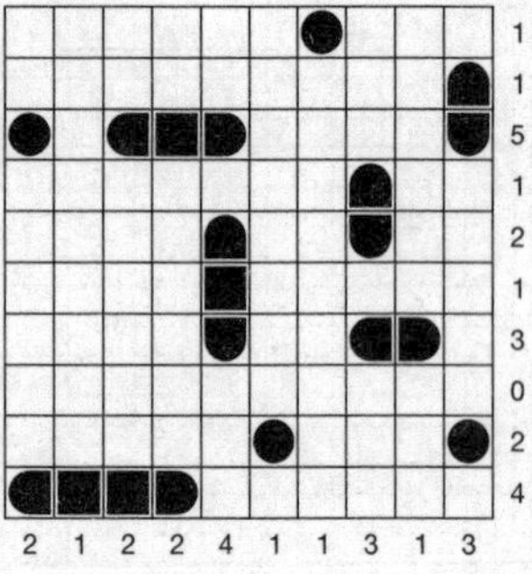

Page 59

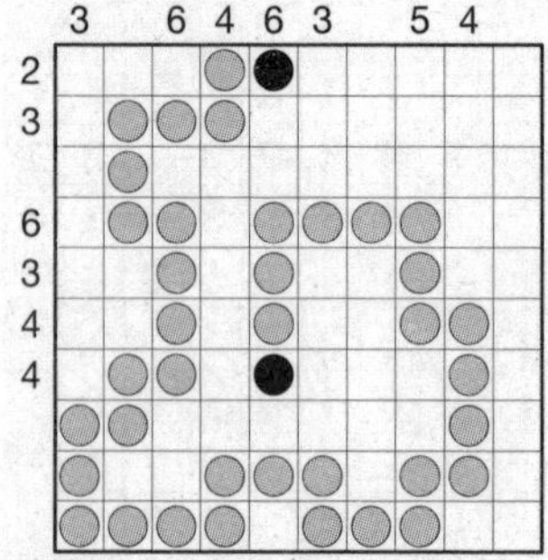

Page 60

7	9	2	8	4	3	6	5	1
1	6	8	9	5	2	7	4	3
3	5	4	1	6	7	2	9	8
6	2	3	4	9	8	1	7	5
4	8	1	6	7	5	3	2	9
5	7	9	2	3	1	8	6	4
8	1	5	7	2	4	9	3	6
9	4	7	3	8	6	5	1	2
2	3	6	5	1	9	4	8	7

▪ Solutions ▪

Page 61

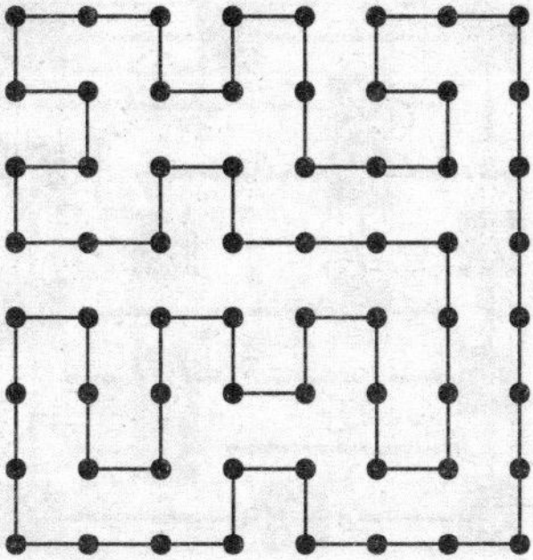

Page 62

30× 6	5	9+ 1	19+ 2	3	4
6× 3	2	5	24× 6	4	1
17+ 2	0– 4	3	5× 1	5	6
4	6	2	12+ 5	1	3
1	18× 3	6	4	10× 2	5
5	1	4	3	4– 6	2

Page 63

1	6	0	5	4	4	4	0
4	3	3	6	6	0	4	2
3	1	1	2	1	5	5	6
3	2	6	6	5	2	1	4
0	5	3	2	2	0	5	0
1	5	4	3	0	6	6	0
1	4	2	3	3	1	5	2

Page 64

64	62	57	52	51	50	46	45
63	61	58	56	53	49	47	44
60	59	4	54	55	48	43	41
6	5	3	1	34	33	42	40
7	10	2	29	32	35	36	39
11	8	9	28	30	31	37	38
12	14	17	18	27	26	22	23
13	15	16	19	20	21	25	24

Page 65

			4			
	5	4	2	3	1	
4	2	1	3	4	5	
4	1	3	4	5	2	
	3	2	5	1	4	
	4	5	1	2	3	2
		1			3	

Page 66

O	X	X	O	O	X	X	O
X	O	O	X	X	X	O	X
O	X	X	O	X	X	X	O
O	X	O	O	X	O	O	O
O	X	O	X	O	X	X	O
X	O	O	O	X	O	X	X
X	O	X	X	O	X	X	O
X	X	O	O	O	X	O	X

▪ Solutions ▪

Page 67

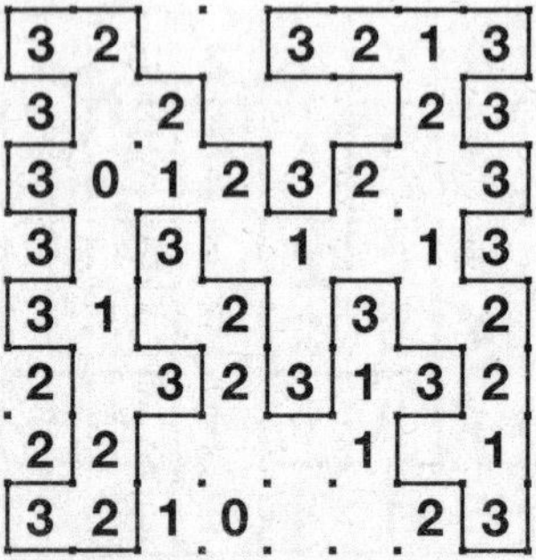

Page 68

Page 69

You buy four apples at 30p per apple. You buy three bananas at 50p per banana. You buy six oranges at 20p per orange.

Page 70

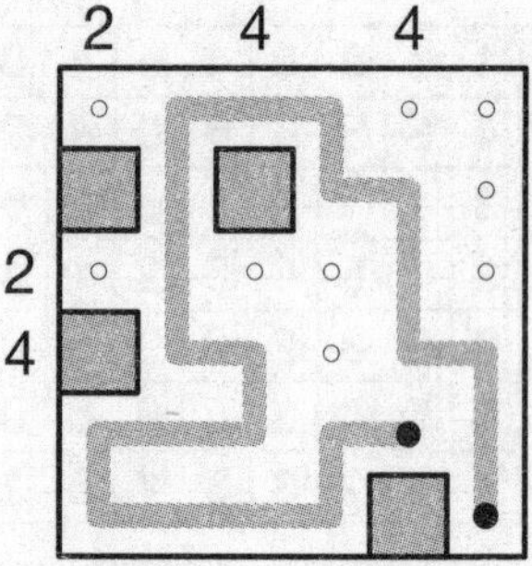

Page 71

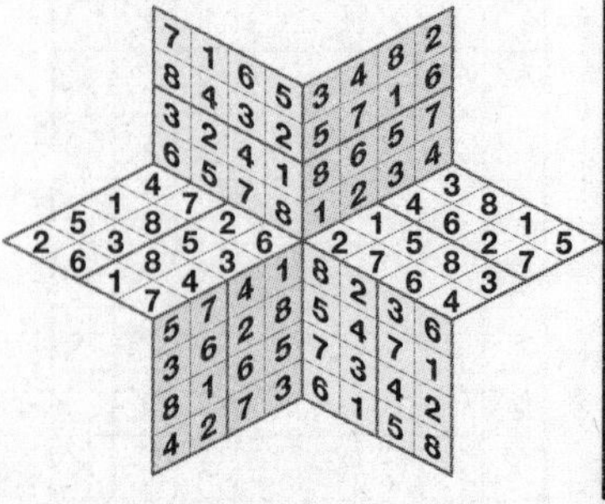

Page 72

▪ Solutions ▪

Page 73

D	G	A	H	B	F	E	C
F	E	C	G	A	H	B	D
A	H	B	D	C	E	F	G
B	C	E	A	F	G	D	H
G	D	F	B	H	C	A	E
C	A	H	E	D	B	G	F
E	F	D	C	G	A	H	B
H	B	G	F	E	D	C	A

Page 74

	5	10	6	3	10	8	
8	3	4	1	2	6	5	13
13	2	6	5	1	4	3	8
6	1	2	3	4	5	6	15
15	6	5	4	3	1	2	6
13	4	3	6	5	2	1	8
8	5	1	2	6	3	4	13
	9	4	8	11	5	5	

Page 75

0	1	0	0	1	0	1	1
0	0	1	0	1	0	1	1
1	0	1	1	0	1	0	0
0	1	0	0	1	0	1	1
1	0	1	1	0	1	0	0
0	0	1	0	1	0	1	1
1	1	0	1	0	1	0	0
1	1	0	1	0	1	0	0

Page 76

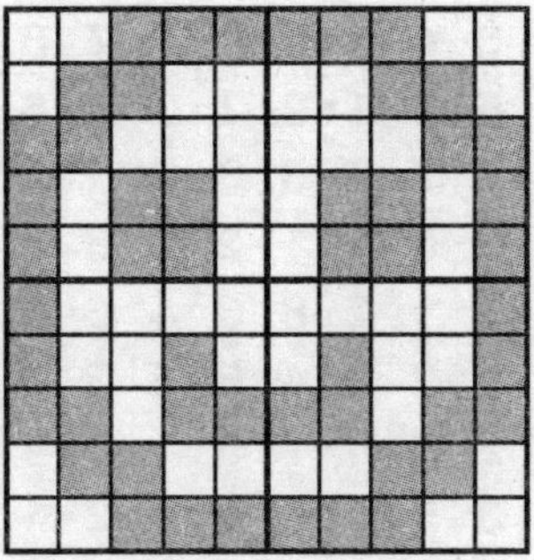

Page 77

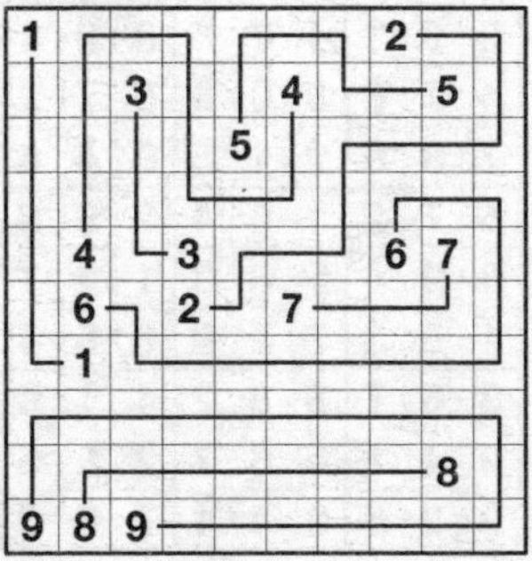

Page 78

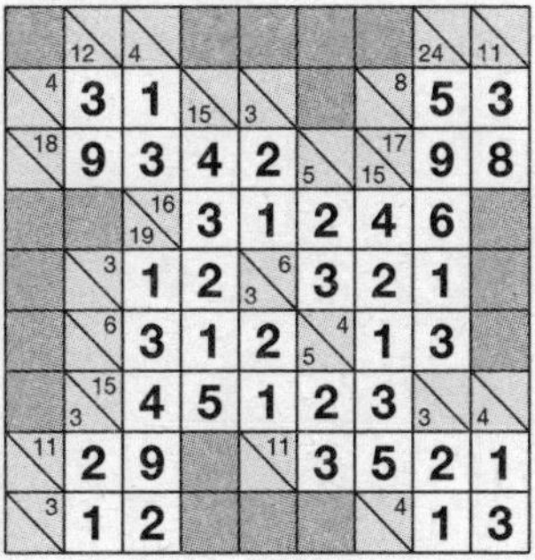

▪ Solutions ▪

Page 79

3	8	7	9	5	2	4	6	1
6	9	5	7	1	4	2	3	8
4	2	1	6	8	3	7	5	9
2	4	9	5	3	1	6	8	7
5	1	8	2	7	6	9	4	3
7	3	6	8	4	9	5	1	2
8	6	4	3	9	7	1	2	5
1	7	3	4	2	5	8	9	6
9	5	2	1	6	8	3	7	4

Page 80

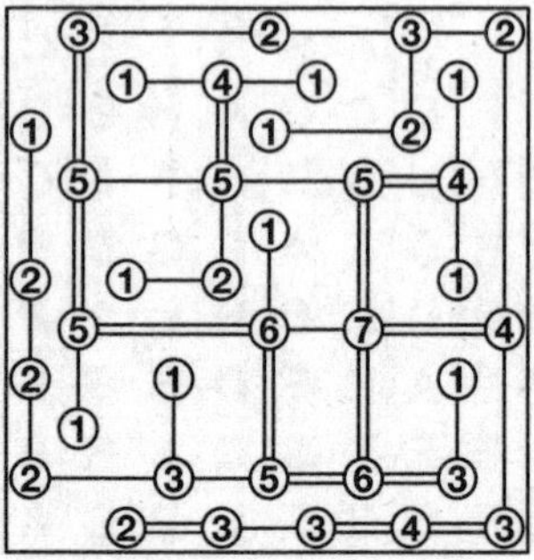

Page 81

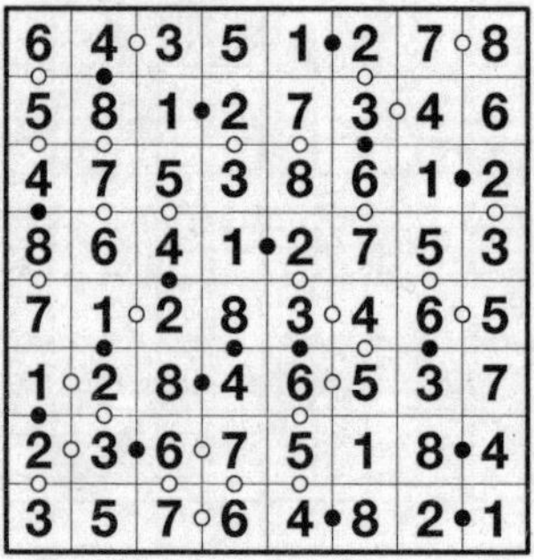

Page 82

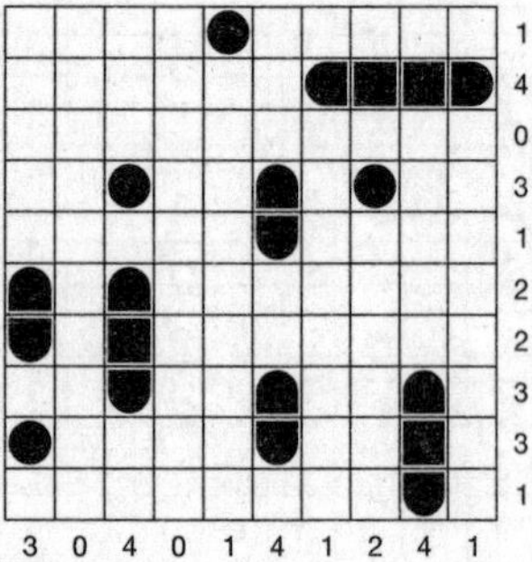

Page 83

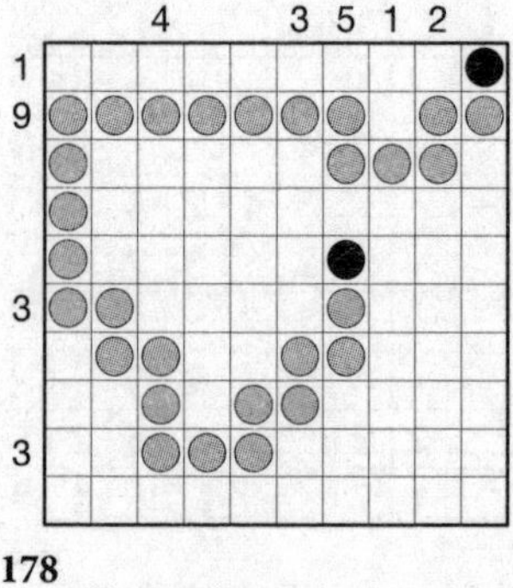

Page 84

2	5	9	4	7	6	8	3	1
4	1	6	3	9	8	5	7	2
7	3	8	2	1	5	9	4	6
5	7	2	1	6	4	3	9	8
6	9	4	5	8	3	1	2	7
1	8	3	7	2	9	6	5	4
3	6	7	8	5	2	4	1	9
9	4	1	6	3	7	2	8	5
8	2	5	9	4	1	7	6	3

▪ Solutions ▪

Page 85

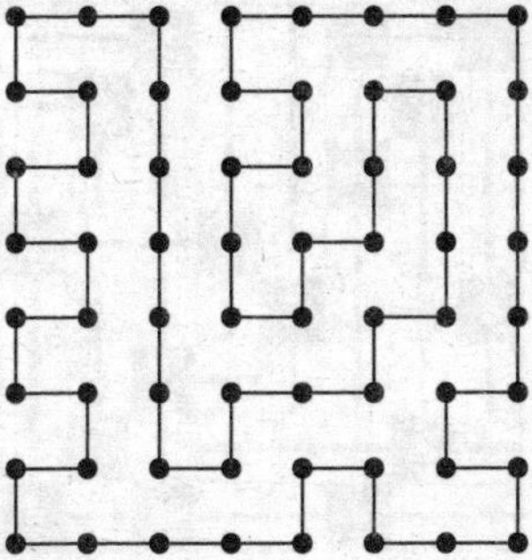

Page 86

4− 2	4+ 1	7+ 4	3	1− 6	5
6	3	0− 1	10× 5	2	1− 4
60× 4	5	6	5+ 2	3	1
3	3− 2	5	16× 1	4	6
5	3− 6	3	4	4− 1	6× 2
4÷ 1	4	3÷ 2	6	5	3

Page 87

5	0	4	5	5	0	0	0
3	3	3	2	1	2	6	2
6	0	3	4	6	4	1	5
2	2	6	4	0	0	1	5
4	1	5	1	4	2	1	5
3	3	1	4	6	2	1	3
3	0	6	2	6	6	5	4

Page 88

27	28	15	14	13	12	11	10
26	29	24	16	17	18	8	9
50	25	30	23	21	7	19	5
51	49	54	31	22	20	6	4
52	53	48	55	32	57	1	3
46	47	42	33	56	58	59	2
45	43	41	37	34	63	62	60
44	40	39	38	36	35	64	61

Page 89

				4	4	
1	5	3	4	1	2	
	4	5	2	3	1	
	2	1	5	4	3	3
4	1	2	3	5	4	
	3	4	1	2	5	1
	3	2				

Page 90

○	○	×	○	×	×	×	○
○	×	○	×	×	○	○	○
○	×	○	×	○	×	×	×
×	○	○	○	×	×	×	○
○	○	×	○	×	○	○	○
○	×	○	○	×	×	○	×
×	×	○	×	○	×	×	○
×	○	○	×	○	×	×	○

▪ Solutions ▪

Page 91

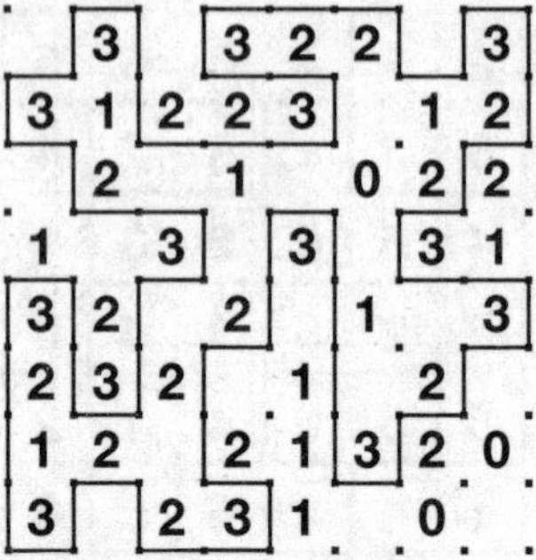

Page 92

Page 93

Your meeting with your boss is on Wednesday at 10am. Your meeting with a client is on Monday at 5pm. Your meeting with your team is on Tuesday at 2pm.

Page 94

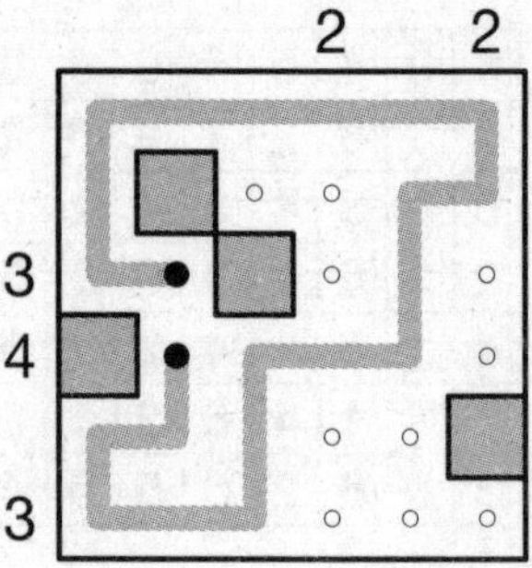

Page 95

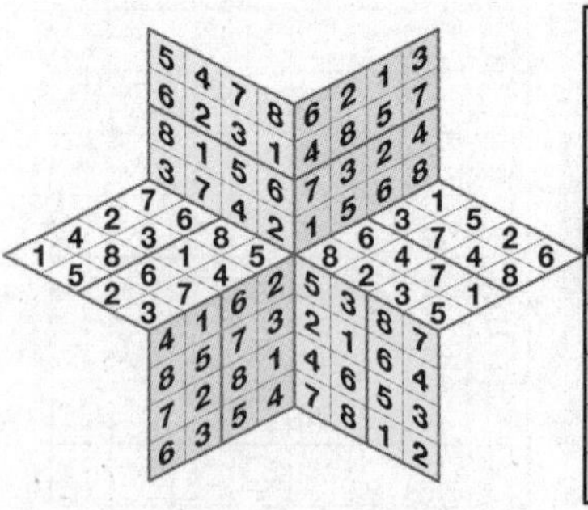

Page 96

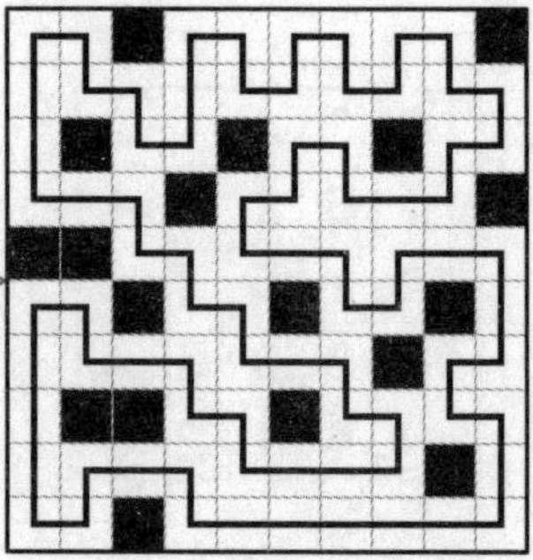

▪ Solutions ▪

Page 97

F	A	B	D	G	H	C	E
H	D	C	E	F	B	A	G
C	E	A	B	D	G	H	F
A	G	D	H	E	F	B	C
B	H	F	G	C	A	E	D
G	C	E	A	H	D	F	B
D	F	H	C	B	E	G	A
E	B	G	F	A	C	D	H

Page 98

	4	8	9	4	8	9	
14	3	6	5	1	2	4	7
7	1	2	4	3	6	5	14
7	4	1	2	5	3	6	14
14	5	3	6	4	1	2	7
7	2	4	1	6	5	3	14
14	6	5	3	2	4	1	7
	8	9	4	8	9	4	

Page 99

1	0	1	0	0	1	0	1
0	0	1	0	1	0	1	1
0	1	0	1	1	0	1	0
1	0	1	1	0	1	0	0
1	1	0	0	1	0	0	1
0	1	0	0	1	0	1	1
0	0	1	1	0	1	1	0
1	1	0	1	0	1	0	0

Page 100

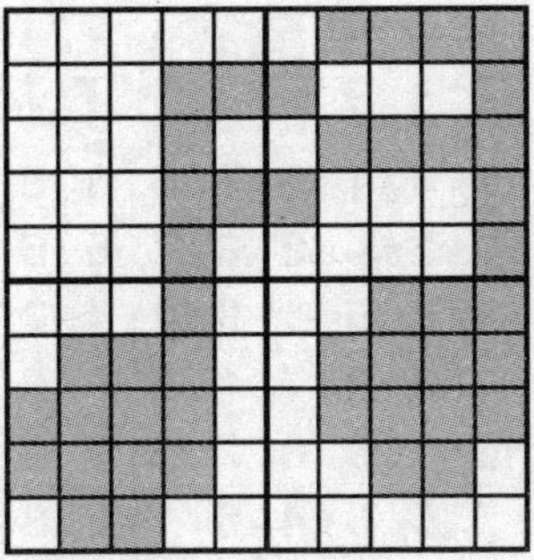

Page 101

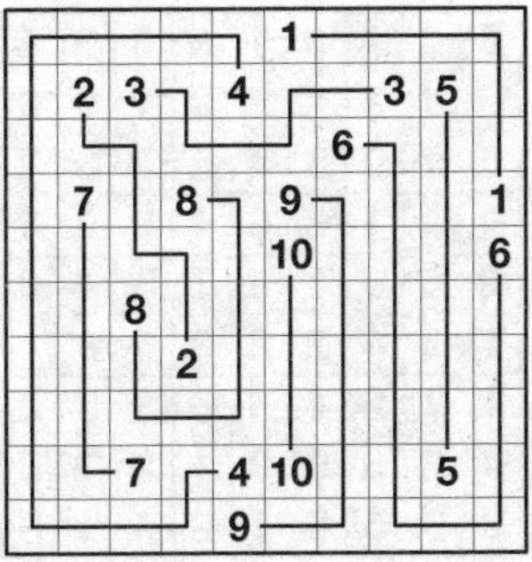

Page 102

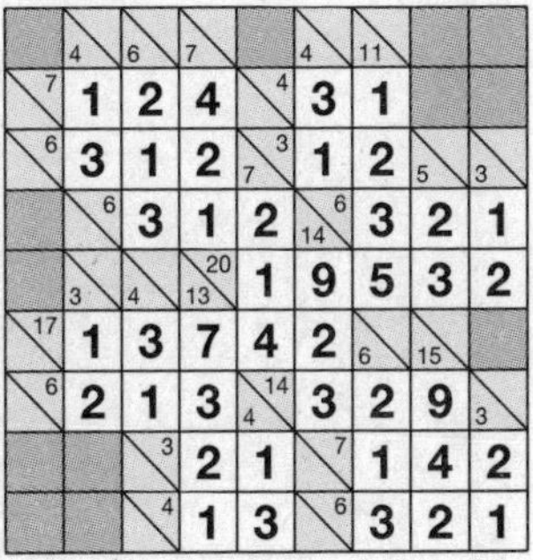

▪ Solutions ▪

Page 103

2	1	5	6	7	9	8	4	3
8	4	7	2	3	1	9	6	5
9	6	3	8	5	4	1	7	2
7	2	4	1	6	5	3	8	9
3	8	1	4	9	7	5	2	6
5	9	6	3	8	2	4	1	7
4	3	2	9	1	6	7	5	8
1	5	8	7	2	3	6	9	4
6	7	9	5	4	8	2	3	1

Page 104

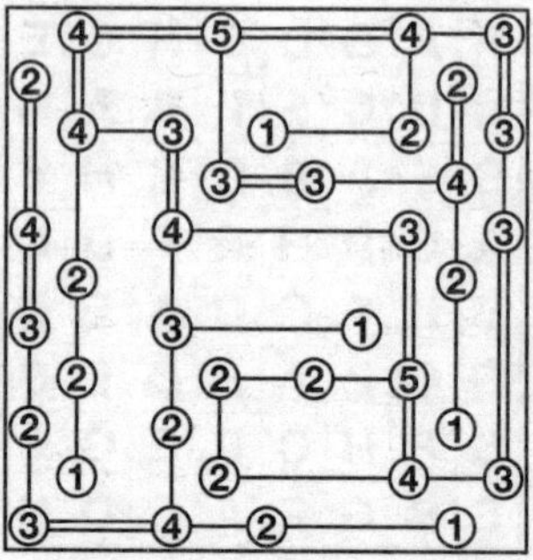

Page 105

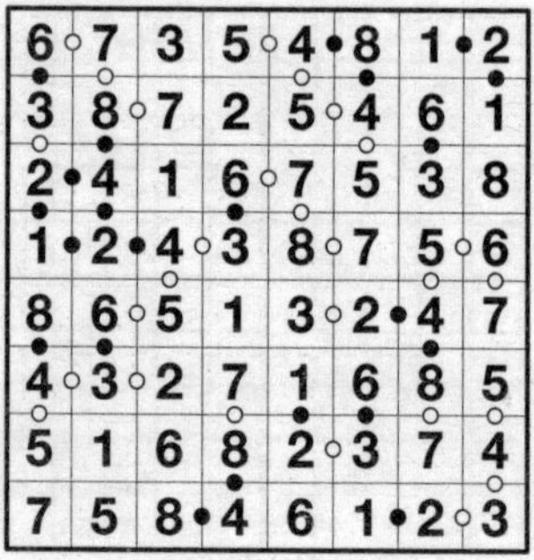

Page 106

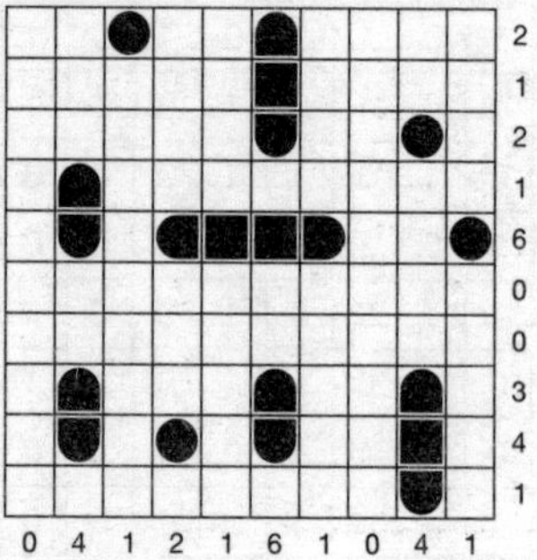

Page 107

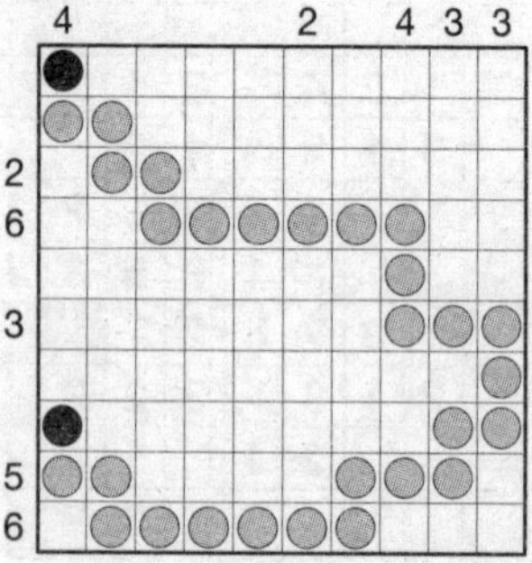

Page 108

8	2	7	3	1	6	9	5	4
5	4	3	7	2	9	1	8	6
6	1	9	8	4	5	7	3	2
9	3	1	5	6	4	8	2	7
2	6	8	1	9	7	5	4	3
7	5	4	2	8	3	6	9	1
1	7	2	4	5	8	3	6	9
4	8	6	9	3	1	2	7	5
3	9	5	6	7	2	4	1	8

▪ Solutions ▪

Page 109

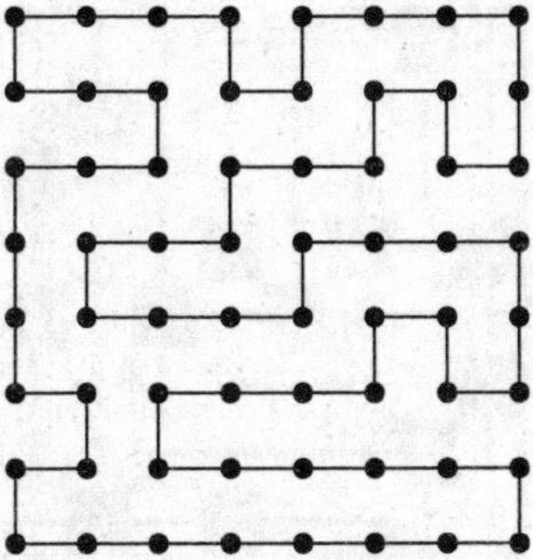

Page 110

1− 3	4	6× 6	50× 5	1	2
10× 2	8+ 6	1	12× 4	3	5
5	2	10+ 3	72× 6	4	1
96× 1	5	2	3	8+ 6	2− 4
4	2− 3	5	2× 1	2	6
6	1	4	2	15× 5	3

Page 111

0	5	6	2	2	0	5	1
3	0	0	2	3	2	6	4
1	2	4	5	0	6	6	4
1	5	3	4	0	2	6	5
1	5	2	4	5	5	6	3
6	6	1	4	4	0	1	3
1	4	1	3	3	0	2	3

Page 112

17	19	15	12	13	8	7	6
18	16	20	14	11	30	9	5
24	21	22	28	29	10	31	4
25	23	27	36	52	34	32	3
48	26	37	51	35	53	33	2
47	49	50	38	62	63	54	1
44	46	42	39	64	61	58	55
45	43	41	40	60	59	56	57

Page 113

		4		3		
	4	1	5	3	2	3
3	3	2	1	4	5	
	1	4	2	5	3	
	2	5	3	1	4	
	5	3	4	2	1	4
	1					

Page 114

O	O	X	X	X	O	X	X
X	X	O	O	O	X	O	O
X	O	X	O	X	O	X	O
O	X	X	O	X	O	O	O
X	X	O	X	O	X	O	X
X	O	X	X	O	X	O	X
X	O	O	O	X	X	X	O
O	O	X	X	X	O	O	O

▪ Solutions ▪

Page 115

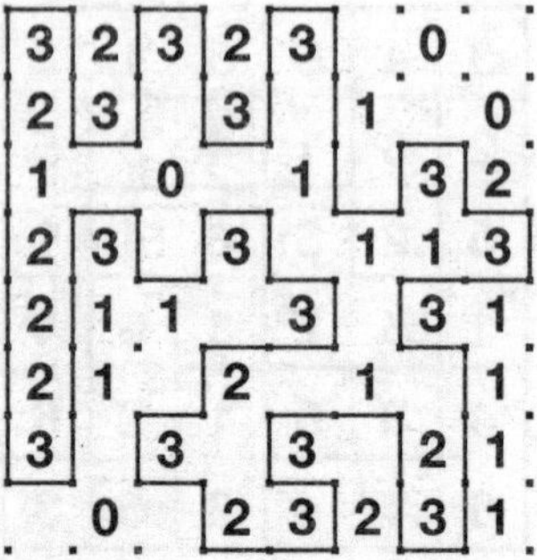

Page 116

Page 117

The train on platform 1 is going to Seatown at 16:00.
The train on platform 2 is going to Sandville at 15:10.
The train on platform 3 is going to Shellbury at 15:40.

Page 118

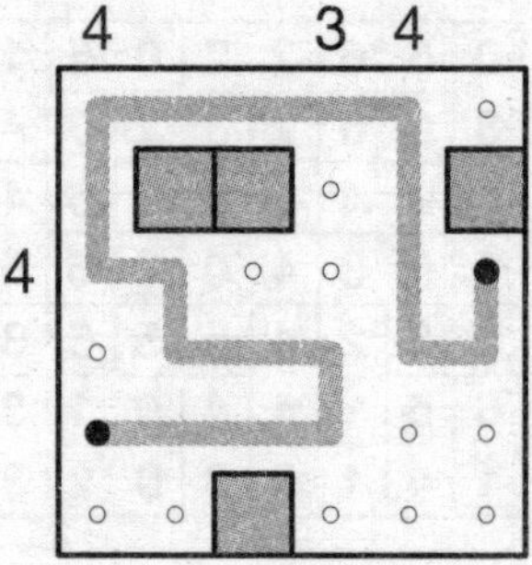

Page 119

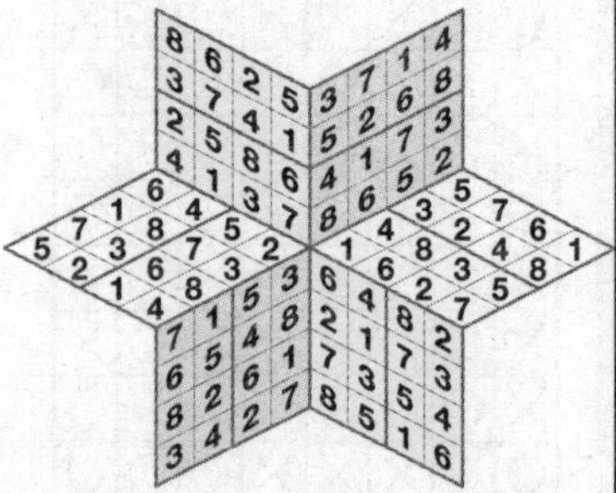

Page 120

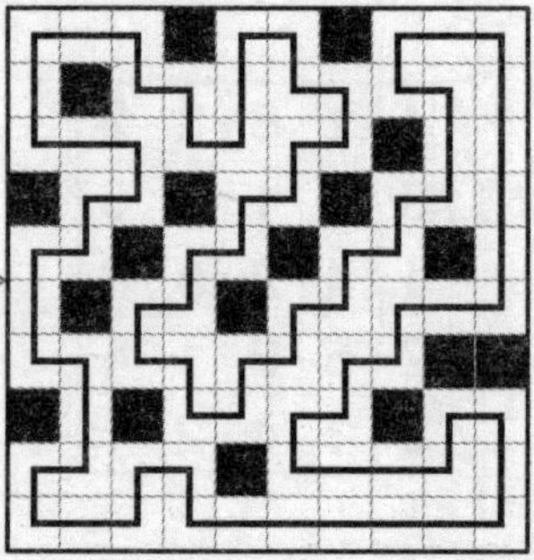

▪ Solutions ▪

Page 121

D	G	F	B	H	E	C	A
B	C	H	G	D	A	F	E
A	D	B	F	E	G	H	C
G	F	E	H	C	B	A	D
C	B	A	D	F	H	E	G
E	H	G	C	A	D	B	F
F	A	D	E	B	C	G	H
H	E	C	A	G	F	D	B

Page 122

	9	3	9	5	10	6	
13	**6**	**2**	**5**	**3**	**4**	**1**	8
8	**3**	**1**	**4**	**2**	**6**	**5**	13
6	**2**	**3**	**1**	**6**	**5**	**4**	15
15	**4**	**5**	**6**	**1**	**2**	**3**	6
7	**1**	**4**	**2**	**5**	**3**	**6**	14
14	**5**	**6**	**3**	**4**	**1**	**2**	7
	6	10	5	9	4	8	

Page 123

0	0	1	0	1	0	1	1
1	0	1	0	0	1	0	1
0	1	0	1	1	0	1	0
0	0	1	1	0	1	1	0
1	1	0	0	1	0	0	1
0	0	1	0	1	1	0	1
1	1	0	1	0	0	1	0
1	1	0	1	0	1	0	0

Page 124

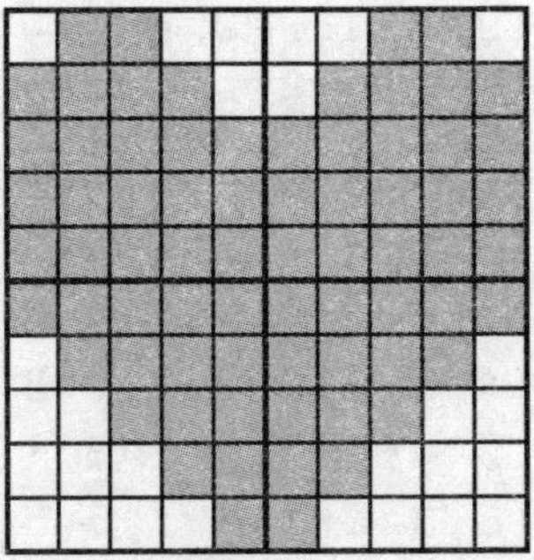

Page 125

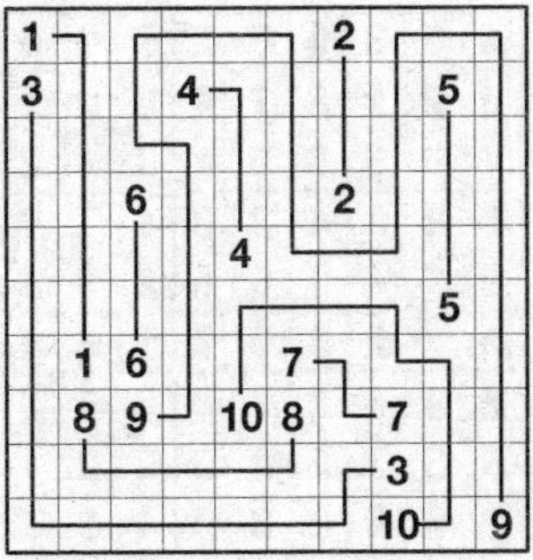

Page 126

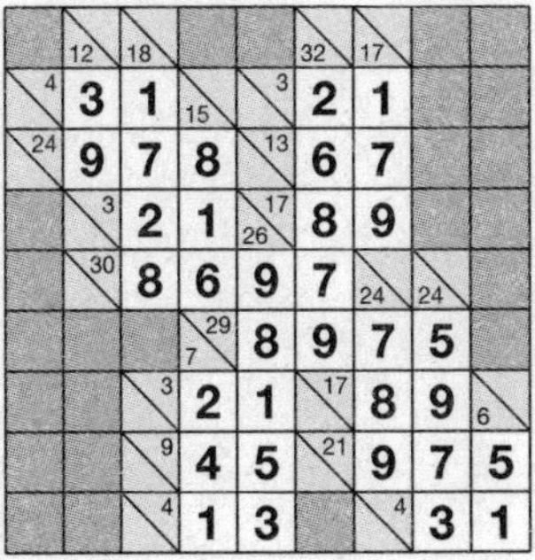

▪ Solutions ▪

Page 127

3	6	4	9	1	5	2	8	7
2	5	9	8	7	4	6	3	1
8	1	7	2	6	3	4	9	5
6	9	1	5	4	8	3	7	2
4	7	2	3	9	1	5	6	8
5	8	3	6	2	7	1	4	9
9	3	5	4	8	2	7	1	6
1	2	8	7	3	6	9	5	4
7	4	6	1	5	9	8	2	3

Page 128

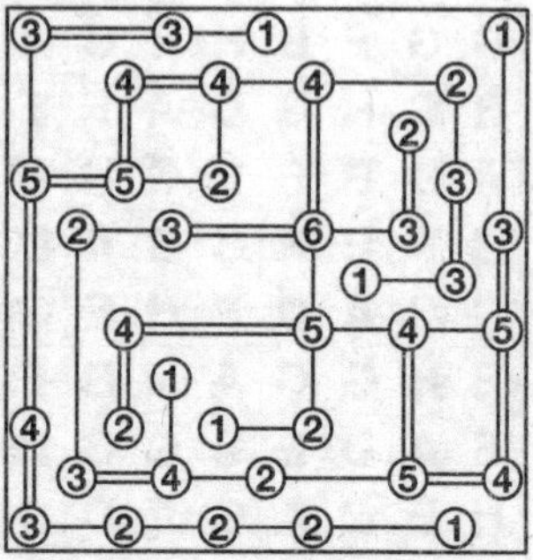

Page 129

6	2	4	5	3	8	1	7
1	7	3	6	8	5	2	4
7	5	6	8	1	3	4	2
2	8	1	4	7	6	5	3
3	1	7	2	5	4	8	6
4	6	5	3	2	1	7	8
5	4	8	7	6	2	3	1
8	3	2	1	4	7	6	5

Page 130

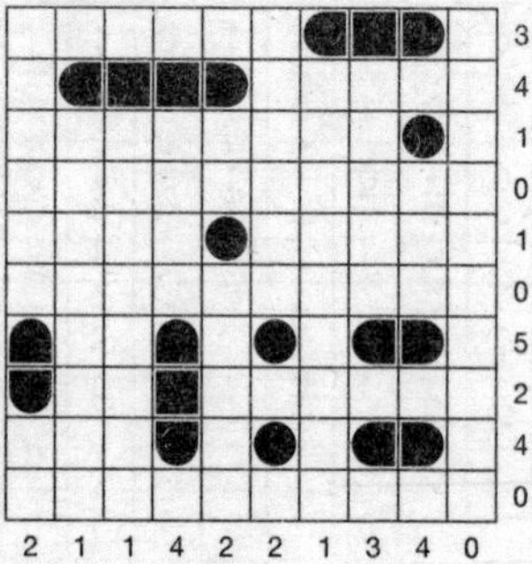

Page 131

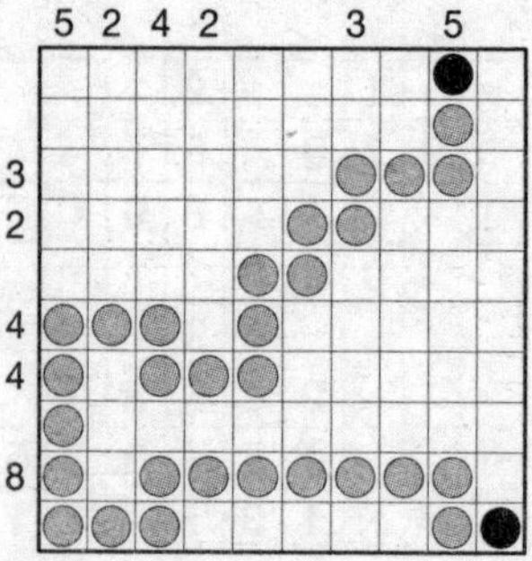

Page 132

4	5	3	9	8	2	7	1	6
6	2	1	3	7	4	8	9	5
7	9	8	6	5	1	3	4	2
5	8	6	4	2	3	1	7	9
9	7	4	1	6	5	2	3	8
3	1	2	8	9	7	5	6	4
2	4	9	7	1	8	6	5	3
8	3	7	5	4	6	9	2	1
1	6	5	2	3	9	4	8	7

▪ Solutions ▪

Page 133

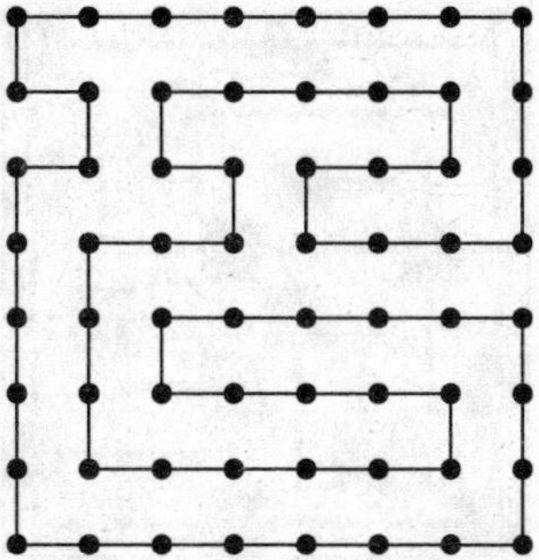

Page 134

14+ 6	5	6× 1	3	2	15+ 4
3	8× 2	4	1	5	6
6+ 1	12× 3	9+ 5	4	9+ 6	1− 2
5	4	3÷ 2	6	3	1
2÷ 2	1	17+ 6	20× 5	4	15× 3
4	6	3	2	1	5

Page 135

5	5	3	2	3	5	4	4
1	3	4	2	6	0	6	6
5	6	4	2	2	6	4	0
0	0	6	1	4	5	4	5
2	6	1	3	3	1	6	1
0	3	2	0	1	5	2	1
0	2	0	5	1	3	3	4

Page 136

64	2	3	10	9	8	28	29
1	63	61	4	11	7	27	30
59	60	62	12	5	6	26	31
58	57	15	14	13	23	25	32
56	17	16	21	22	24	33	34
54	55	18	20	47	40	41	35
53	50	19	48	46	42	39	36
52	51	49	45	44	43	37	38

Page 137

		2	3			
	2	1	3	5	4	
	4	5	2	1	3	2
1	5	3	1	4	2	
4	1	2	4	3	5	
	3	4	5	2	1	3
				4		

Page 138

O	X	O	X	O	X	X	X
X	X	X	O	X	O	O	X
X	O	O	O	X	O	O	O
X	X	X	O	O	X	O	X
O	O	X	X	X	O	X	O
X	X	X	O	X	O	X	O
X	X	O	O	X	O	O	X
O	O	X	O	O	X	X	O

▪ Solutions ▪

Page 139

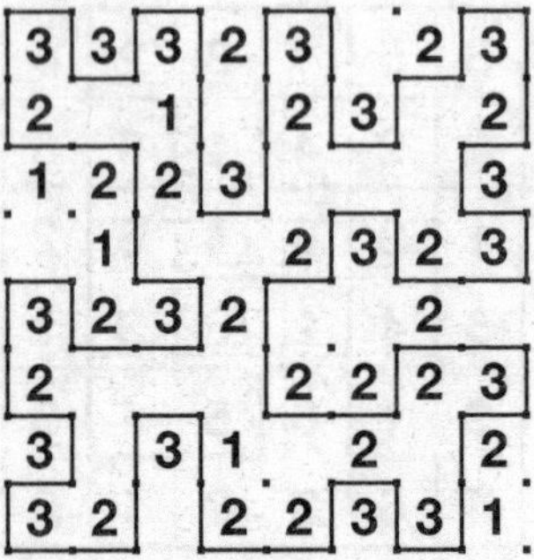

Page 140

Page 141

You eat three cookies with coffee at breakfast. You eat five cookies with orange juice at lunch. You eat two cookies with milk at dinner.

Page 142

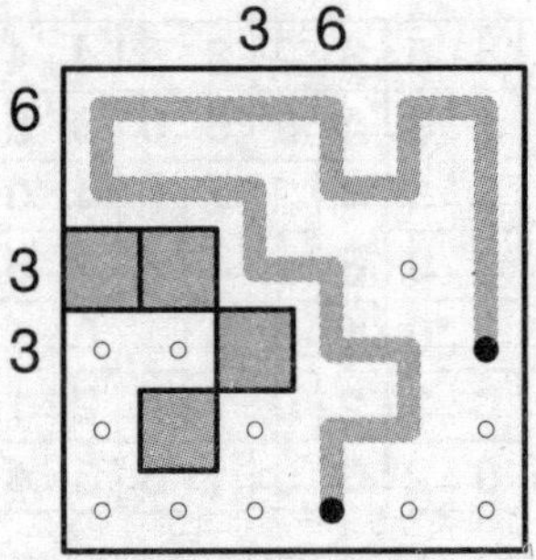

Page 143

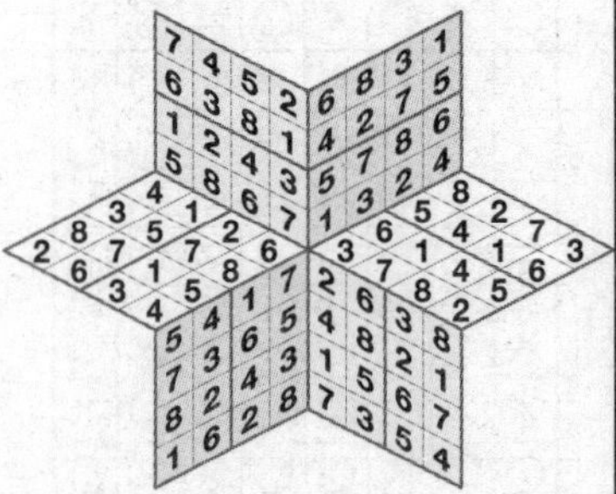

Page 144

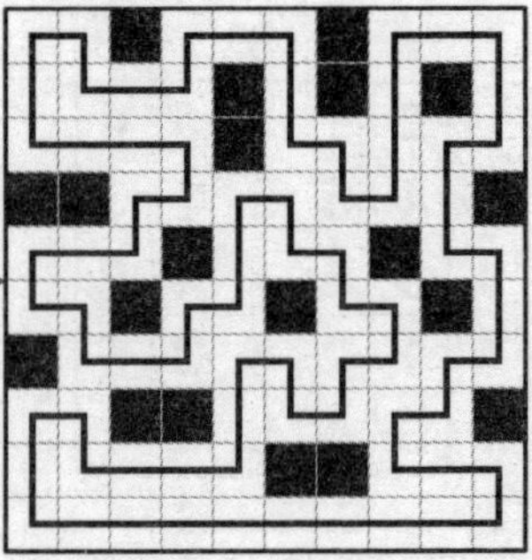

▪ Solutions ▪

Page 145

B	E	F	D	C	A	G	H
A	D	C	G	B	H	F	E
H	G	B	A	F	E	C	D
E	A	H	C	G	D	B	F
D	C	E	B	A	F	H	G
G	F	D	H	E	B	A	C
C	H	A	F	D	G	E	B
F	B	G	E	H	C	D	A

Page 146

	8	6	7	4	11	6	
8	5	2	1	3	6	4	13
13	3	4	6	1	5	2	8
8	1	5	2	4	3	6	13
13	4	6	3	5	2	1	8
8	2	1	5	6	4	3	13
13	6	3	4	2	1	5	8
	8	4	9	8	5	8	

Page 147

0	1	0	0	1	0	1	1
1	0	1	0	1	1	0	0
0	0	1	1	0	1	0	1
0	1	0	1	1	0	1	0
1	0	1	0	0	1	0	1
0	0	1	0	1	0	1	1
1	1	0	1	0	1	0	0
1	1	0	1	0	0	1	0

Page 148

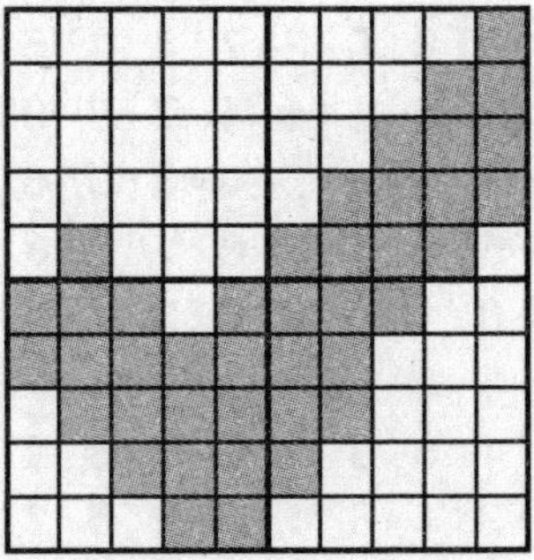

Page 149

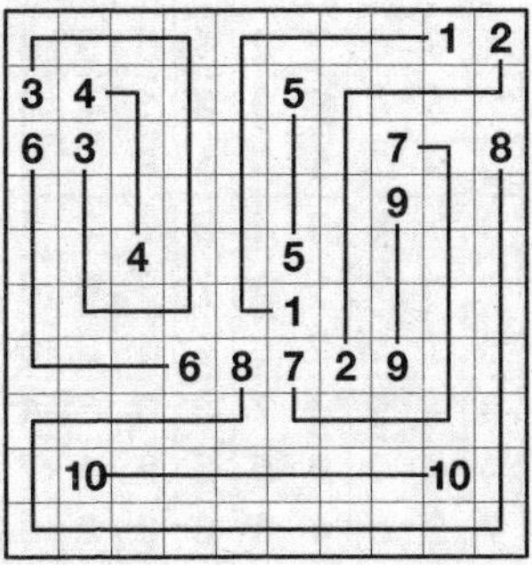

Page 150

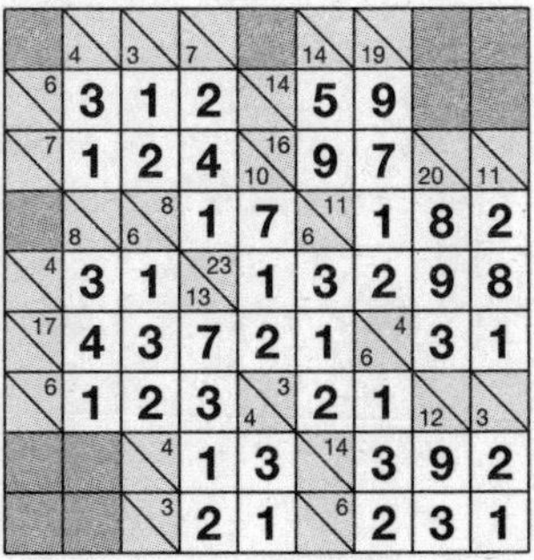

▪ Solutions ▪

Page 151

9	2	5	4	7	1	6	3	8
4	8	1	6	2	3	7	5	9
7	3	6	8	9	5	1	4	2
8	5	3	7	1	9	4	2	6
2	4	7	5	3	6	9	8	1
6	1	9	2	8	4	3	7	5
5	6	2	9	4	7	8	1	3
3	9	4	1	5	8	2	6	7
1	7	8	3	6	2	5	9	4

Page 152

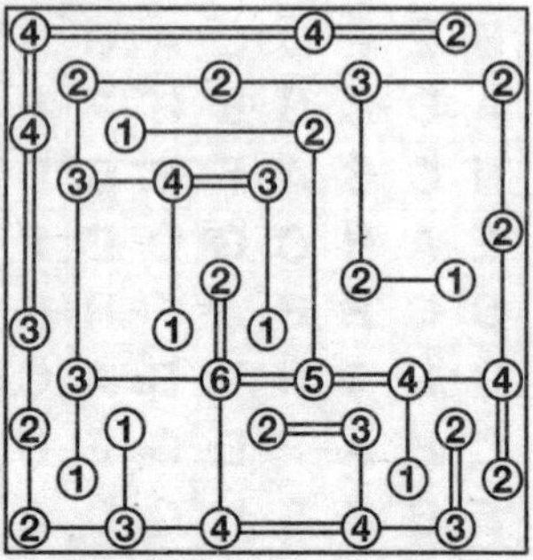

Page 153

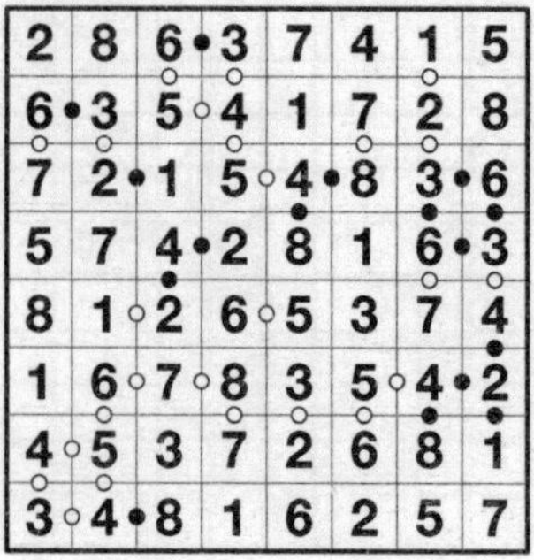

Page 154

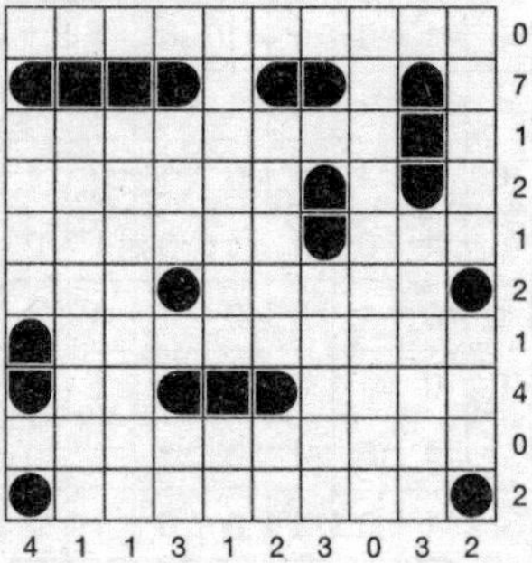

Page 155

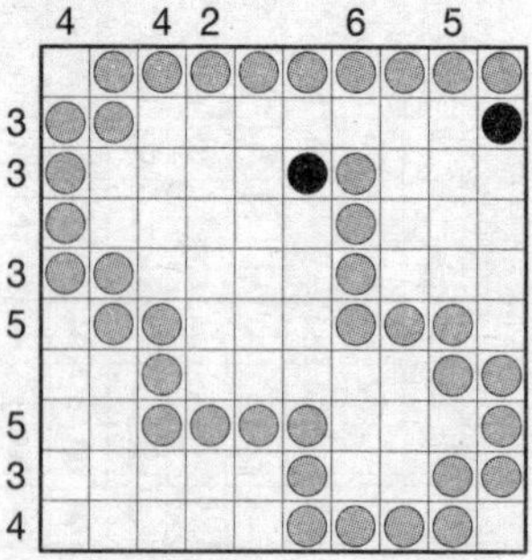

Page 156

1	8	6	7	2	4	5	9	3
2	5	4	8	9	3	1	7	6
3	9	7	5	6	1	8	4	2
9	3	8	6	4	5	7	2	1
5	4	2	1	3	7	9	6	8
6	7	1	2	8	9	4	3	5
8	1	9	3	7	2	6	5	4
4	6	3	9	5	8	2	1	7
7	2	5	4	1	6	3	8	9

▪ Solutions ▪

Page 157

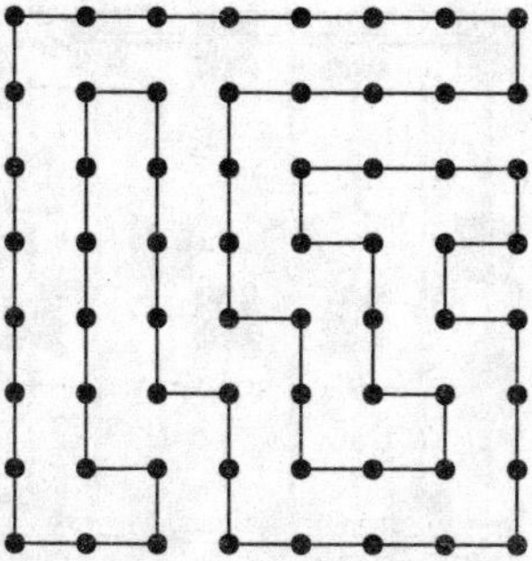

Page 158

4× 4	5− 6	1	2− 2	2− 5	3
1	18+ 5	2	6	7+ 3	4
2÷ 6	1	5	3	4	3− 2
3	96× 2	4	1	6	5
15× 5	3	72× 6	4	2	6÷ 1
2− 2	4	3	5× 5	1	6

Page 159

5	2	1	1	0	4	5	1
5	0	6	3	3	2	0	1
0	0	3	0	3	3	0	3
2	2	2	4	3	4	6	4
6	0	6	2	2	5	4	6
5	1	4	1	6	1	6	3
1	5	5	2	6	4	4	5

Page 160

43	42	40	32	33	30	28	26
44	39	41	34	31	29	25	27
45	38	36	35	10	24	22	20
46	47	37	11	9	23	19	21
48	49	5	8	12	14	15	18
50	4	3	6	7	13	16	17
51	53	2	55	57	58	61	62
52	1	54	56	59	60	64	63

Page 161

		1		2		
	3	5	1	4	2	
4	1	2	4	3	5	
	4	1	2	5	3	
3	2	3	5	1	4	
	5	4	3	2	1	5
				2		

Page 162

X	O	O	X	O	O	X	O
O	O	O	X	O	X	O	O
O	O	O	X	X	X	O	O
O	X	X	O	O	X	X	X
X	O	O	X	X	O	O	X
X	X	O	O	O	X	X	X
O	O	X	X	X	O	O	O
X	X	O	O	X	O	O	O

▪ Solutions ▪

Page 163

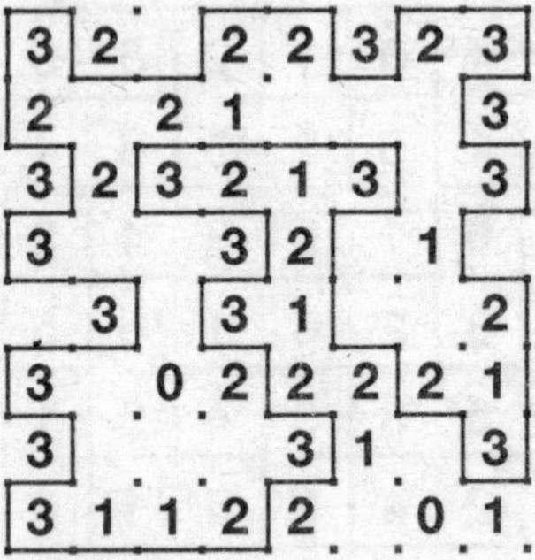

Page 164

Page 165

Today it will be 10° with hail. Tomorrow it will be 20° with rain. The day after tomorrow it will be 17° with clear skies.